"If you're serious about
today, and their legacy
instruction book. Based
merous interviews with grandparents, and strong work with the
leading grandparenting ministry in the country, this is an important resource whether you have one or eleven grandchildren."

—John Trent, PhD, president of StrongFamilies.com;
Gary D. Chapman Chair of Marriage, Family Ministry,
and Therapy, Moody Theological Seminary

"When grandkids come, we enter into one of the most important
seasons of ministry for the Lord Jesus. I have always looked forward to being a grandfather. Now, after reading *Grandparenting*, I
am more excited than ever before! This book is packed with biblical principles and practical approaches that God will use to deepen
and accelerate your ministry to the generations of your family."

—Dr. Rob Rienow, founder of Visionary Family Ministries

"If you are a grandparent or soon to be one like me, get a copy
of this book! In *Grandparenting: Strengthening Your Family and
Passing on Your Faith*, Josh Mulvihill offers page after page of
inspiration to help grandparents be more than cheerleaders. As a
grandparent, you'll gain a vision to help your grandchildren know,
love, and serve Jesus and get the practical wisdom you need to put
those goals into practice."

—Marty Machowski, pastor and author
of *Long Story Short: Ten-Minute Devotions to Draw Your
Family to God*, *Parenting First Aid*, and *The Ology*

"What Josh Mulvihill provides here takes a significant step in the
direction of developing a new vision for grandparents in our families. This book is packed with solid biblical foundations. Read this
work carefully, constantly seeking ways you can be more effective

as a disciple-maker in the lives of your grandchildren and in the life of the church."

—Timothy Paul Jones, PhD, associate vice president for the Global Campus, the Southern Baptist Theological Seminary

"Dr. Josh Mulvihill is an outstanding advocate and supporter of grandparents. His research delivers new insights for grandparents. Josh's book *Grandparenting: Strengthening Your Family and Passing on Your Faith* is a road map for grandparents who seek creative ways to pass on their faith to their grandchildren. Dr. Mulvihill's writing is tempered in biblical truth, which will inspire you in your grandparenting journey."

—Ken Canfield, president of the National Association for Grandparenting

Grand Parenting

Grand Parenting

Strengthening Your Family and Passing on Your Faith

DR. JOSH MULVIHILL

BETHANY HOUSE
a division of Baker Publishing Group
Minneapolis, Minnesota

Published by Bethany House Publishers
11400 Hampshire Avenue South
Bloomington, Minnesota 55438
www.bethanyhouse.com

Bethany House Publishers is a division of
Baker Publishing Group, Grand Rapids, Michigan

Printed in the United States of America

ISBN 978-0-7642-3126-1

Library of Congress Control Number: 2018940479

Cover design by Dan Pitts

Author is represented by William Denzel.

18 19 20 21 22 23 24   7 6 5 4 3 2 1

CONTENTS

FOREWORD

It is a rare grandparent I encounter today who didn't fully delight in the day the first grandchild arrived. Yet when asked what being a grandparent means, they reveal that much of what they believe is rooted more in culture than in Scripture.

What do today's cultural messages, formed mostly in narcissism and materialism, reflect about your view of grandparenting, and how does that compare with what God says in the Bible?

I received a T-shirt not long after becoming a grandparent for the first time. It read,

GRANDPA'S TO-DO LIST

1. Spoil 'em
2. Fill 'em up with sugar
3. Send 'em home

I suspect you might have smiled when you read that, partly because you identify with this fiendish cultural view of grandparenting. Still, deep inside, does it unsettle you because you sense there must be something more to grandparenting? If it does, you would be right. Being a "good" grandparent who enjoys your grandchildren and loves making them feel good is not enough. Because God has something more to say about it.

That's what this book is about.

I have met few people in my travels who have a more profound grasp of the biblical role of grandparenting than Josh Mulvihill does. His wisdom is certainly molded by his own experiences as a pastor in children's and family ministry, and as a father, son, and grandson. It is also rooted in a vigorous commitment to study and research. But mostly, it is born of wisdom shaped by a commitment to the Gospel of Jesus Christ. It is driven by his desire to help grandparents like you and me put into practice what God says in the Bible about grandparenting.

Believe it or not, the notion that grandparents play a strategic role in the character and faith development of a child is rare. It is not even on the radar screen of most grandparents I have met over the past two decades. Fortunately, because of people like Josh—a dear friend and colleague—that is beginning to change.

Josh takes on the undercurrent of cultural lies that have swept many of us up in their wake. He does it not to chastise us (though God knows we need it), but to reshape our thinking about God's design for family and family discipleship as defined by Scripture. The cultural message of "spoil 'em and enjoy 'em" is only one of the lies that must be called out and replaced with God's truth. You will learn how to do just that if you read and take to heart what Josh has written in this book.

Because you are reading this, I assume you have a desire to be the kind of intentional grandparent God wants you to be, rather than to settle for misguided cultural norms. Josh will guide you to make much of Christ so you can lay the foundation for another generation to know and follow Him. You will be challenged to courageously swim upstream against the culture.

It will require intentionality and commitment to absorb and put into practice what you are about to learn for the sake of your grandchildren. The good news is that God's divine power has already given you everything you need *through Him who has called you by His own glory and goodness* (2 Peter 1:3).

Those of us who are grandparents know there is no greater joy than to see our grandchildren (and children) walking in the truth. Josh is about to lead you on a journey of discovery and faith that can lead to such joy. It is a journey that will empower you to build a legacy that is truly worth outliving you—one for which your children and grandchildren will call you "blessed," and the Father will say, "Well done, good and faithful servant" (Matthew 25:21).

When your grandchildren come to your funeral, will they only remember the good times they had with you? Or will they praise God because your life smelled of the fragrance of Jesus and the all-satisfying delight of knowing Him?

Your legacy matters only when the truth of the Gospel is what matters first and foremost.

Josh is right: "Grandparenting exists to deliver the Gospel to future generations."

—Cavin T. Harper
Founder and President,
Christian Grandparenting Network

INTRODUCTION

God designed grandparents to be disciple-makers who pass on a rich heritage of faith in Christ to future generations. Grandparenting is God's idea. He created it, which means grandparenting has an important purpose and a vital function. But if there is one word that summarizes how many people feel about grandparenting, it's *help*!

Grandparenting is filled with many joys, but it also comes with many challenges. Family dynamics are complex, technology is always changing, and children are busy. Broken families, fractured relationships, and prodigal children cause the heart to ache. In the midst of all these challenges, grandparents have to figure out how to navigate unstated family expectations and the unexpected state of the family.

In addition, grandparents have been marginalized by society and ignored by churches. Churches undervalue, under-resource, and underutilize grandparents. And the result? Many Christian grandparents are unclear what the Bible teaches on the subject, and often live lives that are emotionally distant and disengaged from their families.

God is at work awakening the church and families to the important role grandparents have in passing on the Gospel to future generations. Grandparents have the opportunity to shape the beliefs of future generations, strengthen the family, build the church, and transform the nation. Imagine the impact of millions of Christian grandparents intentionally making disciples of children and grandchildren.

Due to longer life expectancy, the opportunity for grandparents to spiritually invest in their grandchildren's lives has never been greater. Despite the opportunity, the impact of grandparent investments may have never been smaller than it is today. It's time we changed that for the glory of God and the good of our family.

After reading this book you should

- recognize and reject the powerful cultural messages about grandparenting;
- understand the biblical role of a grandparent;
- learn how to disciple children and grandchildren by practicing eight biblical methods of discipleship; and
- strengthen family relationships by looking to the Gospel to shape practices and solve problems.

The Need

A number of years ago, when I began a PhD program in family ministry, my initial discoveries about the lack of resources for Christian grandparenting were shocking. I found

- zero in-depth biblical studies on grandparenting;
- one ministry to equip Christian grandparents (the Christian Grandparent Network led by Cavin Harper);
- one small-group or Sunday school DVD series on grandparenting;

- seven books on grandparenting published in the past fifteen years (not counting gift books or grandparenting journals).

I discovered that there are millions of Christian grandparents with limited training and resources. Everywhere I looked I saw a huge need.

I also saw the potential influence that millions of equipped grandparents could have in the lives of children, families, churches, and society for the sake of Christ.

As a pastor, my vision was to help my local church minister more effectively to families. God had bigger plans than one local church and connected me with Cavin Harper and Larry Fowler. Together, with a team of wonderful friends, we have launched the national grandparenting ministry the Legacy Coalition, published a growing number of resources on grandparenting, and started grandparenting ministries in churches all over the country. If you would like to read the results of my research, they are available in the book *Biblical Grandparenting*, and additional family discipleship resources are available at gospelshapedfamily.com.

The content of this book is the culmination of my PhD research, a full year of studying the Bible from cover to cover to learn what it had to say about grandparenting, and interviews with grandparents from all over the country.

By God's grace, grandparents are being awakened to their God-designed role, church leaders are beginning to understand the value of grandparents in the spiritual lives of children, and children have another influence to help them know Christ and grow in spiritual maturity.

The Sufficiency of Scripture for Grandparenting

If you search the market, you will find a growing number of books on grandparenting, but you will have a difficult time finding one that teaches you how to be a grandparent based on the Bible. That's what makes this book different from the rest. My goal is to help you understand and apply what the Bible says about grandparenting.

The Bible is sufficient for all of life, including grandparenting. To call the Bible sufficient means that if all we had was the Bible, it would be enough on its own to teach us how to grandparent. It means that the Bible is the primary source and authority for grandparenting and that other sources are secondary and supplementary.

The Bible has a lot to say about grandparenting.[1] God defines the role of grandparents and He describes the methods to pass faith to future generations. God didn't call grandparents to a task without telling them how to accomplish it. We will explore that in this book.

Grandparents Matter

I find that many grandparents underestimate the impact of their life on grandchildren. I want you to reject the lie that claims your best days are behind you and your greatest value is to dispense large amounts of sugar to grandchildren. By God's design, your influence is powerful and your presence matters.

I can speak to the value of grandparents because I have experienced what it is like to not have a grandmother's Gospel-rich influence on my children. My mother died from ALS (amyotrophic lateral sclerosis) when my oldest child was one, and a few years later my mother-in-law died from brain cancer. Do grandparents matter? Absolutely. Their deaths and absence made parenting more difficult.

God blessed the Mulvihill family and gave my children a new grandmother, whom we call Grammie Pammie. Pam has been God's gift to our family, and a wonderful grandmother. One of the unexpected joys of my life was officiating my dad and Pam's wedding. How many sons get to officiate their dad's wedding?! My dad and Pam are intentional grandparents who teach the truths of God's Word, woven in and out of the times they spend with grandchildren. I can also say that grandparents matter because I watch my children's personalities, preferences, and passions in life being shaped by their grandparents.

Overview of the Book

This book contains four sections: Cultural Messages, God's Design, Discipleship Practices, and Strengthening Relationships. We will explore the strong but subtle messages culture communicates that threaten to neutralize your spiritual influence. We will also study what the Bible says about the role of grandparents and examine the methods God created to disciple future generations so that you are equipped to pass on a rich heritage of faith in Christ. We conclude with a section to help you strengthen relationships with your family.

Each section ends with a chapter from grandparents that I admire and encourage you to emulate—Valerie Bell, CEO of Awana; Cavin Harper, president of the Christian Grandparent Network; and my dad and Pam, grandparents of sixteen grandchildren. Each story is unique, but there are common threads running through them. You will notice that each of them recognized and rejected cultural messages, made a commitment to be a disciple-maker who passes on a heritage of faith, and intentionally invested in the lives of their grandchildren. I want you to be encouraged by their examples and inspired to be a biblical grandparent. The book closes with a Grandparent Declaration written by Larry Fowler, founder of the Legacy Coalition, and you will have the opportunity to commit to being an intentional, disciple-making grandparent.

Let me ask you a weighty question: Would it make any *spiritual* difference to your children and grandchildren if you were no longer alive?

Death has a way of clarifying what matters most and helps to eliminate the vanities from life. The thought of our own death reminds us what is most important and encourages us to make the most of the time we have. One of the good things that came from the death of my mom and mother-in-law was a heightened awareness of the spiritual value of grandparents in my children's lives.

If you are a grandparent who is living for something other than Jesus Christ, then let this be your invitation to use the final third of your life to make an eternal impact for the Gospel. It is never too late, and you are never too old.

If you feel like you've blown it, this book will help.

If you need practical ideas, you will find them in these pages.

If you don't know how to rebuild a relationship with an adult child, I will point you to Jesus, the only person who can restore relationships.

If you want to see your children, grandchildren, and great-grandchildren walking with Christ, I will teach you the biblical principles God has given for this purpose.

PART 1

CULTURAL MESSAGES

1

Influencing Grandchildren for Christ

A Life That Reflects Christ in Every Way

Patt's seventeen-year-old granddaughter was struggling with her faith, so Patt planned an outing that centered around three spiritual lessons in hopes of strengthening her granddaughter's faith in Christ. Many months after that outing, Patt received the following text from her granddaughter:

> I have learned more about how to be a Christian by watching how you live your life. The way you pursue a life that reflects Him in every way, whether that be through your marriage or simply talking to a man in a restaurant. For seventeen years I have watched you share the gospel shamelessly and point our family toward Him. In every situation good and bad I have ever been in, you have reminded me that it is not about me and that I serve a God that has a plan for me that ultimately leads to Him. The day we spent going around to different landmarks reading that book is what I attribute the beginning of my spiritual journey to. You showed me that following Him is all that matters.

A life that reflects Christ in every way. What a powerful testimony and an aim for each of us. Praise God for grandparents like

23

Patt. God used Patt to draw her grandchild to Christ and pass faith to future generations. What if Patt had not purposefully nurtured her granddaughter's faith? What path might her granddaughter have taken in life?

Patt is an example of a spiritually influential grandparent because she did two things: She lived a Christlike life worthy of imitation, and she was intentional. Notice how Patt's granddaughter watched her grandmother and was deeply impacted by a sincere faith consistently lived out over time. Patt was attuned to her granddaughter's spiritual state, recognized she was struggling with doubts, and purposefully invested in her granddaughter's spiritual life.

If this were your granddaughter, would you recognize her spiritual struggle? Equally important, how would you respond? Think for a moment about your grandchildren. Do you know how they are doing spiritually? Has your grandchild placed faith in Jesus? Is your grandchild growing spiritually, or is he or she stagnant? What are the trials and temptations your grandchild is facing?

I've never met a Christian grandparent who doesn't want their grandchildren to love Jesus, but I've met plenty of grandparents who lack a biblical focus and the proactive intentionality to encourage that result.

After talking with hundreds of grandparents, I am convinced that the majority of Christian grandparents would benefit from a clear understanding of their role as well as a big-picture biblical vision that guides what they do with children and grandchildren on a daily basis. If you've never thought deeply about the role you play in a grandchild's life, this book will help you understand the why, what, and how of grandparenting according to the Bible.

Identifying the Source

What is the source of your understanding of the role of a grandparent? While there are likely many, the three most common sources I have observed are:

- *Grandparents.* Your own grandparents' lives were powerful. They shaped you. From their positive or negative impact you formed ideas about the role of a grandparent. Your beliefs may or may not be correct. I have found that many individuals have not thought critically about their beliefs or compared them with the Bible's teaching on grandparents. Often, Christian grandparenting practices are a replication or rejection of a person's experience with grandparents. Your grandparents' success or failure should not be the benchmark for your understanding of grandparenting.

- *Culture.* Many Christian grandparents have been significantly impacted by a cultural view of grandparenting. Christian grandparents have integrated portions of society's views, even while attempting to follow Christ. The result is that grandparents have been extra, nonessential members of the family with a minimal role spiritually.

- *The Bible.* It has a lot to say about grandparenting, and God's Word is clear and compelling. Intentionality and conviction will come as we take our cues about grandparenting from the Bible. Before picking up other books on grandparenting, pick up the Bible and learn what God has to say about the topic.

We each look to an authority on grandparenting. The authority we choose determines what we believe and how we operate as grandparents. Maybe you picked up this book for grandparenting guidance and, if so, I'm glad you did. My job is to explain what God says about grandparenting in the Bible. God's ways are always the best ways and lead to the best results.

Four Roles Christian Grandparents Embrace

One of the primary barriers that limits a grandparent's spiritual impact with grandchildren is uncertainty about the role of a grandparent. This section will help you understand the four most common roles Christian grandparents embrace, and encourage you to move from aimless activity to purposeful grandparenting so that you can seize teachable moments, capture lost opportunities, and pass on a rich heritage in Christ to future generations.

My goal is to equip you to be an intentional grandparent who raises children and grandchildren who treasure Jesus. In order to do that, you need to assess your personal beliefs about the role of a grandparent. I have asked grandparents what they understand their role to be, and I summarize the responses in these four categories:[1]

Encouraging Voice: A cheerleader who loves grandchildren for who they are and the unique giftings they possess. This grandparent sees the positives, and desires to bring out the potential in their grandchildren. Seeks to help grandchildren accomplish goals and has a tendency to ask questions and listen. If this role were summarized as a book title, it would be *The Power of a Positive Grandparent: Helping Your Grandchildren Reach Their Full Potential*.

Supportive Partner: A helping hand with the day-to-day tasks of parenting. This grandparent operates as a co-laborer who comes alongside their adult children in a variety of ways. Oriented toward seeing and meeting a need. An agreeable grandparent who reinforces their children's parenting practices and philosophies without interfering. If this role were a book title, it would be *101 Ways You Can Help Your Adult Children*.

Loving Friend: A companion whose focus is building a strong relationship with grandchildren and having fun together. Often avoids difficult conversations or disciplinary matters. An activity-oriented grandparent who likes to create memories, communicate affection, and occasionally spoil grandchildren. If this role were a book title, it might be *Fun! The Key to Your Grandchild's Heart and Happiness*.

Disciple-Maker: A mentor who intentionally attempts to pass faith in Christ to future generations. Desires to see their grandchild know Christ and grow in Christ. Seeks to live as a Christlike example and share godly wisdom with grandchildren. If this role were a book title, it would be *How to Help Your Grandchild Know, Love, and Serve Jesus.*

Which of the four roles best describes you as a grandparent? If you had to choose only one, which would it be? Your personality, preference, and family situation will likely impact how you engage as a grandparent, so this may change over time. You may find that with some grandchildren you operate as a helping hand, and with others you are a cheerleader. My hope is that you begin to see your patterns and tendencies as a grandparent and, as we get further into the book, you will be able to compare your understanding and actions with the biblical role of grandparents.

Grandparents often comment that all four categories are important. That is true. However, there is a difference between primary and secondary importance. Some grandparent functions, while important, are support roles that enable a grandparent to accomplish the primary responsibility God has given them. Love, support, and encouragement are important but they are not the end goal of grandparenting. They exist for the greater purpose of passing on faith to future generations.

If you are like three out of four Christian grandparents and your primary role is one of the first three, then there are three things I want you to consider:

1. *You should evaluate your grandparenting goals.* For many Christian grandparents, encouragement, support, or love are the end goal rather than a means to intentionally helping grandchildren mature in faith. Supporting adult children is important. Encouraging grandchildren is valuable. There is a place for fun activities. But if these actions don't have a

greater purpose and encourage grandchildren to treasure Christ, then they fall short of God's purpose for us as grandparents. What is success for you as a grandparent? What are you hoping to accomplish in the life of your grandchildren?

2. *You should recognize the difference between spiritual intent and spiritual impact.* I've interacted with many Christian grandparents who fall into one of the first three categories and speak about the importance of a grandchild's spiritual growth, but do not grandparent in a way that prioritizes the spiritual growth of the grandchild. On a day-to-day basis, many Christian grandparents are reactive, not proactive. They are fun-centric, not discipleship-oriented. What do your daily grandparenting actions reveal about your grandparenting priority? How have you invested your time as a grandparent over the past month, and what does that suggest about what is most important to you as a grandparent?

3. *You can increase your spiritual influence.* The good news is that you can have a deeper, more substantial spiritual impact on your children and grandchildren. The bad news is that grandparents who operate as encouraging voices, supportive partners, or loving friends typically don't have as significant a spiritual impact as they desire or think they are having. Are you grandparenting in a way that encourages your grandchildren to know, love, and serve Jesus? On a scale of one to ten, how do you rate the spiritual influence you have on your grandchildren?

I urge every grandparent who primarily operates as an encourager, support, or companion to act with greater purpose and more intentionality to pass faith in Christ to future generations. It is no accident that you are a grandparent. God believed you were the right grandparent for the job and has uniquely equipped you to influence your children and grandchildren for Christ. One of the first steps to helping your grandchildren know, love, and serve Jesus is to understand the potential influence you can have in their lives.

Grandparents Are Influential

Who are the most influential people in a young person's life? A Barna study wanted to know the answer to a similar question and asked 602 teenagers, "Who, besides your parents, do you admire most as a role model?"[2] According to Barna, the top five influences in the life of young people are (1) parents, (2) other family members, typically grandparents, (3) teachers and coaches, (4) friends, and (5) pastors or religious leaders.

After parents, grandparents are the greatest potential influence in the life of a child—not a peer, not a pastor, and not a teacher. When teenagers were asked why they named a particular person as influential, teens provided the following reasons: The person was worthy of imitation; they wanted to follow in the footsteps of the chosen person; they were there for the teenager; and they were interested in the teenager's future. For better or worse, young people are imitating the people they know best and who care for them.

It may sound simplistic, but the greatest influencers of young people are typically those who invest the greatest amount of time into their lives. The key for grandparents to understand is that the more time you invest into a grandchild's life, the greater the potential influence will be. When I look at Barna's top five influences it follows that logic: The five greatest influencers are the people who spend the most time with young people over the course of their life.

If you want to influence your grandchildren to love Jesus, then it makes sense that you must have an active presence in their lives. If you do not, then other influences such as peers or media fill the void. Take a moment and reflect on two areas of your life:

First, add up the numbers of hours you invest monthly in your grandchildren.

- How much of that time is face-to-face interaction (in person or through technology)?
- How many hours per month do you invest indirectly in your grandchildren's parents, praying for grandchildren, preparing for gatherings, activities, or other family-related things?
- What is your total number of hours?

Many grandparents are surprised to see how few or how many hours they actually spend on their grandchildren.

Second, take a moment and think about your own grandparents.

- What impact did your grandparents have on your life?
- Were your grandparents active in your life and did they regularly invest in you?
- Did your grandparents shape your personality, preferences, or faith in any way, or were your grandparents emotionally distant, primarily living an autonomous life?

Whether the impact was significant or lacking, it reminds us that grandparents matter, and rarely do they have no influence on us. If you ask your grandchildren how you influence their life, what do you think they would say? The goal is not simply to be a positive influence with a strong relationship, but to use our influence to point grandchildren to Christ.

An Abundance of Counselors

Young people need an abundance of counselors. The Bible teaches, "Where there is no guidance, a people falls, but in an abundance of counselors there is safety" (Proverbs 11:14). This is true for your grandchildren. God created parents as the first and primary disciple-makers, and grandparents are second. Your grandchildren need as many godly counselors in their life as possible, and God is calling you to actively step into this role.

One of the enemy's tactics is to isolate Christians from one another so they are vulnerable to discouragement and deception. This is true of families today who strongly value the American ideal of individualism. One of the major problems that must be addressed is the underlying belief that immediate family and extended family are two individual entities best kept separate. We'll explore the individualistic mindset and where that came from in the next chapter, but for now I simply want to draw your attention to it.

Young people mature best in Christian community where they are doing life with wise and seasoned Christians. It has been said that it takes a village to raise a child. According to God, it takes a family to raise a child, which includes parents and grandparents. God created the home as the first Christian community for the purpose of nurturing the faith of future generations. Disrupt or destroy the home and it directly impacts the passing of the Gospel to future generations.

Grandparents are one more voice, one more example, one more influence to raise children to treasure Jesus, and it is my hope that you embrace your God-designed role with Gospel-intentionality and a Christlike influence. How do you do that? That is what we will explore in the second section of this book. But first, it is important to understand the cultural messages that limit a grandparent's spiritual influence.

Grand Chat

1. Of the four roles mentioned, which role best describes you? Why?

2. Many grandparents identify with two of the four roles and of those, one is primary and one is secondary. Which role describes you in a secondary way?

3. Which role least describes you?

4. How do you define success as a grandparent? What are you hoping to accomplish in the life of your grandchildren?

5. How have you invested your time as a grandparent over the past month, and what does that suggest about what is most important to you as a grandparent?

2

Recognizing Culture's Role for Grandparents

Three Messages Every Grandparent Must Reject

Craig approached me with a big smile on his face and asked if I wanted to see a picture of the vegetable drawer in his refrigerator. His mischievous smile told me that I wouldn't see carrots or lettuce. "Sure," I said, intrigued by what I would find. Craig pulled out his phone and showed me a picture of a fully extended vegetable drawer that was half filled with full-sized candy bars of all varieties. "I love to feed my grandchildren vegetables, and they love to eat them," he said with a chuckle.

While there is nothing wrong with feeding grandchildren "vegetables," have you ever asked yourself where this idea of grandparenting comes from? Who decided that a grandparent's job description includes spoiling grandchildren with large amounts of sugar?

The truth is that Craig longs to be a good grandparent. He loves his grandchildren and he wants them to love Jesus. But without realizing it, Craig's approach to grandparenting has been strongly influenced by the values of society rather than being informed by

Scripture, and as a result, his grandparenting focuses on fun rather than purposeful grandparenting.

Christian grandparents face a major challenge: *American culture communicates powerful messages about the role of a grandparent.* Most of those messages are not biblical and will not deliver the results most grandparents desire, such as intimate family relationships and godly grandchildren.

My research revealed that three out of four Christian grandparents operate according to cultural expectations rather than biblical principles. Most grandparents have difficulty articulating the role God has given them (we will explore this in the second section) and are unable to discern the erroneous messages from society about their place and purpose in the home. The combination has been lethal and has led to Christian grandparents who look more like culture than Christ, which in turn has significantly limited their spiritual influence on future generations.

This chapter is an overview of the cultural messages about the role of a grandparent. I want you to familiarize yourself with these messages and begin to pay attention to what you read and hear about grandparenting from culture. Here are three cultural messages Christian grandparents must reject:

1. ***You need to live your life independent of your family.*** You know the warnings. Don't meddle. Don't interfere. Don't overstep. Don't be a burden. Society works hard to convince you that a mono-generational existence is more desirable than a multigenerational life. The essence of this value is seen in a bold statement by an author who declares that she wants little to do with her children and grandchildren as she ages: "We desire to live our lives physically and personally independent of our children."[1] This phrase summarizes grandparenting in the twenty-first century, and its message must be rejected. God does not intend for you to isolate yourself from your family, but to intentionally invest in them.

2. *You've worked hard and now it's time to enjoy yourself.* The world tells you that you did your time and now it is time to rest, travel, and play. The essence of this message is that you are to indulge yourself with whatever makes you happy. The Bible never speaks positively about a self-focused season of life, yet this is what retirement has become for many Christians. Billy Graham writes, "Retirement presents us with two choices: Either we can use it to indulge ourselves, or we can use it to make an impact on the lives of others."[2]

3. *Your role is to be a companion and playmate to your grandchild.* You are told to be the fun grandparent and spoil your grandchildren. This value can manifest itself in many different ways, from high volumes of sugar to extended family vacations at Disney. Fun can be a secondary value, but for many it has become the primary aim. Your grandchild needs his or her sins forgiven more than a good gift and a sugary treat. If you are going to spoil your grandchildren, give them something that won't perish or spoil—the Gospel. Your grandchildren need deep lessons about what matters most in life, and they desire your physical presence more than additional presents. The enemy seeks to kill, steal, and destroy the faith of your children and grandchildren. If your impact is limited to being a playmate, you are doing little to protect your family and prepare them for lifelong faith.

We are met with cultural views of grandparenting at every turn. Mottos like "sugar them up and send them home" reveal the misplaced aims of today's grandparents. I want you to take a moment with me to explore these three cultural messages in greater depth so you can recognize and reject them. All grandparents, including you, have to contend with these ideas and determine if they align with God's design for grandparents or deviate from it.

Meet Del Webb

I want to introduce you to Del Webb. More than likely, you've never heard of him, but you have been impacted by his views about the purpose of retirement and the role of older Americans. Del Webb was a businessman who sold the American Dream to retired individuals, and in doing so reshaped the place and purpose of the elderly in America.

In 1962, *Time* magazine put Del Webb on its cover with the title "The Retirement City: A New Way of Life for the Old."[3] Webb's research suggested that retirees would welcome the opportunity to distance themselves from their families and limit involvement, something once thought impossible. Webb built one of the first retirement communities, located in Arizona, and promised sunshine, low-cost living, and something to do. Webb sold this lifestyle as the new American Dream, suggesting retirees "had worked hard, and now it was time to pursue hobbies, play golf, and socialize with their peers."[4] In 1962, the idea was so revolutionary that *Time* made Webb its Man of the Year. Webb created a new national template for retirement in America that enticed older adults to relocate geographically far away from families and focus on themselves.

Webb's lifestyle proved to be popular and helped to create a new class of people: retirees.

This new phase of life created an identity crisis in which older Americans began to ask what retirement was supposed to look like and what they were supposed to do with the years they had left to live. Grandparents adjusted their value system based on the place and purpose society gave to the elderly. Values shifted from leaving a family legacy and financial inheritance to a pleasant retirement experience. A bumper sticker occasionally seen on the car of elderly people captures this well: "We're spending our children's inheritance." Instead of investing in future generations, older couples are encouraged to "indulge themselves a little, in travel, little splurges, or whatever makes their last years more enjoyable."[5]

The Leisureville Life

Del Webb's vision for life has become deeply rooted in American culture and is clearly recognizable at The Villages. The Villages provides a clear example of two cultural messages communicated to Christian grandparents that you must recognize and reject: *Pursue independence from family, and live a life of indulgence due to years of hard work.*

The Villages is the world's largest retirement community and one of the nation's fastest growing cities. Andrew Blechman, author of *Leisureville*, describes what life is like at the gated retirement community in Florida. The Villages has more than 100,000 residents, spans three counties and two zip codes, and provides everything retirees could desire, including recreation centers, dozens of pools, more than a thousand hobby clubs, countless restaurants, and a golf course for each day of the month.[6] The Villages has been called Disney for adults, where "it's like being on a permanent vacation."[7] Betsy, a resident of The Villages, states, "It's fun. Just plain fun. And why not have a good time? We're retired and we have enough money to live here. We've worked hard for this."[8] Older adults are told that they have earned the privilege of a life of leisure, which has led to a noticeable ambivalence toward future generations and has been one factor to disconnect the generations from one another.

Residents of The Villages prioritize a life of leisure, which looks shockingly similar to a second adolescence. One resident of The Villages states, "We've been here six years and absolutely love it. It's like being a kid again."[9] Roselyn Shelley, a sixty-eight-year-old resident, states, "Whatever you know about twenty-year-olds, it's the same with seniors."[10]

How are the two similar? The teenage years are marked by high levels of freedom with limited responsibility and a life of leisure to pursue personal interests. The older adult years are often marked by these same ideals. The American dream presented to older adults is a vision of life that embodies freedom from responsibility to pursue a life of leisure where retirement resembles a never-ending summer break. Our culture encourages young people to remain in adolescence as long as possible and elderly people to return to it as quickly as possible.

The Villages is missing one thing: children. No one under the age of nineteen may live at The Villages, and visits from grandchildren are limited to thirty days per year. Blechman states, "The Villages provides residents with something else they crave—a world without children."[11] The Villages has legalized the separation of ages and reveals a growing value of American culture: age segregation. Age segregation has a big impact on families and churches, especially as it relates to the transmission of faith from one generation to the next.

Sadly, many Christian grandparents have absorbed the values of a Leisureville life and embraced independence and indulgence. The messages are subtle but strong. The problem with this approach to life is that it is incompatible with God's design for grandparents, removes grandparents from a central role in the family, and neutralizes their ability to transfer faith in Christ to future generations.

The Social Contract

America has created its own role for grandparents; it is known as the social contract. The social contract consists of unspoken expectations one generation has for another that guide interactions and determine relational boundaries. The core values of the social contract include non-interference by grandparents, emotional independence from children, and personal autonomy. Families unconsciously operate according to the agreement that children will grow up, move away, start their own family, and become independent from one another.

What does the social contract sound like? Jim, a Christian grandparent, states, "We don't want to interfere with how our son or daughter-in-law are raising them." Valerie admitted, "I didn't want to step on their parenting toes and mess everything up." Betty's sentiments are similar: "We don't want to intrude, but at the same time we care. . . . We have tried very, very hard not to get into our children's business." Do you notice the common thread? Christian grandparents don't want to "interfere," overstep, or "intrude."

Arthur Kornhaber describes the social contract in this way:

> This family contract designated the principles of emotional and personal independence, autonomy, and no enmeshment with one's family of origin. As a result, many of us lead disconnected lives. This is exaggerated by increased geographical mobility and economic opportunity (moving to where the jobs are for the young and moving to the sun belt for retired seniors). When children come along, and support is needed, we find ourselves independent, autonomous, for sure; but also alone, overburdened, and disconnected.[12]

Experts encourage families to aim for closeness at a distance, but what is gained is lonely, overburdened, and disconnected families. The social contract has amputated generations from one another and left countless grandchildren as grandorphans who do not have the intimate influence of a grandparent in their life.

Grandparents commonly avoid conflict or difficult topics so they don't overstep their boundaries, which may upset children or result in lost privileges. Many grandparents have a difficult time articulating specific boundaries and are foggy regarding what constitutes interference and what does not. For many grandparents, interference is simply what upset their adult children, and many times this would not be known until after the fact. A lack of clarity regarding a grandparent's role commonly leads to timidity, passivity, and fear from grandparents and requires a family-by-family negotiation to define the place and purpose of a grandparent in the home.

Companion and Playmate

How do the values of independence and indulgence shape the role of grandparents today? I've observed three results of this influence.

Wrong goals. What is important *to* a grandparent becomes the focus *of* grandparenting. Self-indulgent individuals make grandparenting about indulging grandchildren. Grandparents who live for their own happiness make the happiness of grandchildren the central aim of grandparenting. How is this accomplished? For some grandparents it is manifested in a permissive posture that ignores rules and avoids correction of grandchildren. For others it takes the shape of lavish gifts or high volumes of sugar. Yet others desire to be seen as the fun grandparent who provides memorable experiences and allows grandchildren to stay up late, eat whatever they want, and consume hours of media. These variations can be summarized by the cultural idea that grandparents exist to spoil grandchildren. Spoiling grandchildren is the anthem American grandparents sing and the target for which they aim. However, it must be rejected as a counterfeit deviation from God's designed role for grandparents.

The clearest expression of the role of a grandparent can be found in children's literature about grandparenthood. If you ever want to understand what culture believes on a subject, listen to what is being communicated to children. A few notable children's books include *Grandmas Are for Giving Tickles* and *Grandpas Are for Finding Worms.* The children's book *What Grandpas and Grandmas Do Best* suggests that grandparents are for playing hide-and-seek, singing a lullaby, building a sand castle, and playing games. In *Grandma, Grandpa, and Me*, grandparents are to play with, work alongside, and have fun with. Children's literature presents a grandparent's role as playmate and companion.

Many Christian grandparents have absorbed the culture's approach to grandparenting with one difference. Most Christian grandparents recognize that grandparenting is more than fun and games and should have a spiritual component to it. For many Christian grandparents, that is prayer. When cultural messages collide with Christian grandparents, out comes a philosophy of grandparenting that is characterized by two duties: *pray* and *play*. Christian grandparents pray when alone and play when with their grandchildren.

Role confusion. In American culture there is uncertainty concerning the meaning and purpose of grandparenting. Ambiguity surrounds the role. Many grandparents, including Christian grandparents, do not know what is expected of them. Gunhild Hagestad, an expert on grandparenting, states, "There is new uncertainty about what it means to be a grandparent and what grandparents are supposed to do."[13] Other experts, Andrew Cherlin and Frank Furstenberg, believe that "there are no clear guidelines on how to be a grandparent."[14] These statements are significant because grandparenting experts believe society does not understand the most basic and most important aspect of grandparenting. The same is true for Christian grandparents, and I want to provide a few examples for you.

As part of my PhD study, I interviewed Christian grandparents from all over the United States and asked them to describe their role as a grandparent. The following are short excerpts taken from those interviews and represent many Christian grandparents today.

- "I'm not sure I have a real good vision for that."
- "I never saw myself as having any kind of role at all as a grandparent."
- "When you contacted me about grandparenting, it was like, wow, I'm not even thinking about these things."
- "We don't know what we are doing. Flying by the seat of our pants because there really isn't anything."

- "I am totally receptive to the idea of being as helpful and engaged in the lives—especially in the spiritual lives—of grandchildren, but I think to some degree grandparents feel unlearned."

Many Christian grandparents confess that they have given little thought to their job as a grandparent and have no plan for passing faith in Jesus to future generations. In general, many Christian grandparents are confused about the role of a grandparent. One of the purposes of this book is to provide a clear explanation of the role God has given grandparents, according to the Bible.

Poor outcomes. If you adopt society's views about grandparenting, you automatically place yourself at the periphery of the family with a minimal role and limited spiritual influence. In general, families have lost their compass regarding why the generations should interact, how they are to do so, and what responsibilities one has to the other. Because the role of grandparent is not clearly defined by American culture, it is viewed as an extra, a role not essential to the functioning of the family or the growth and development of grandchildren. It is critical that you recognize the unbiblical message of culture and reject it so you can

- *Think eternally* in all that you say and do as a grandparent.
- *Act intentionally* because you understand your role and the spiritual outcome God desires for your children and grandchildren.
- *Communicate regularly* to build and maintain a healthy relationship centered on Jesus.
- *Connect deeply* with children and grandchildren for the purpose of passing on a rich heritage of faith in Christ.
- *Love unconditionally* when children or grandchildren make unwise choices or do something hurtful.

- *Pray fervently* with the understanding that it is God who changes hearts and draws grandchildren to himself.

Unfortunately, many Christians have unintentionally adopted an unbiblical view of grandparenthood and need a renewed biblical vision regarding their role in the family and their purpose in society. That is the focus of the next section. But before we explore the biblical role of a grandparent, I want you to hear from Valerie Bell, CEO of Awana, as she shares about grandparenting as a season of giving in chapter 3.

Grand Chat

1. What impact did your grandparents have on your life? How did your grandparents influence you, positively or negatively? Was their impact great or small?

2. Share a favorite memory of your grandparents.

3. How have the following cultural messages impacted your role as a grandparent?

    a. You need to live your life independent of your family.

    b. You've worked hard and now it's time to enjoy yourself.

    c. Your role is to be a companion and playmate to your grandchild.

4. How have you observed Christian grandparents adopting a Leisureville approach to life?

5. Did any of the following statements resonate with you? If so, how?

    a. "I'm not sure I have a real good vision for that."

    b. "I never saw myself as having any kind of role at all as a grandparent."

c. "When you contacted me about grandparenting, it was like, wow, I'm not even thinking about these things."

d. "We don't know what we are doing. Flying by the seat of our pants because there really isn't anything."

e. "I am totally receptive to the idea of being as helpful and engaged in the lives—especially in the spiritual lives—of grandchildren, but I think to some degree grandparents feel unlearned."

3

Giving Season

BY VALERIE BELL, CEO OF AWANA

Recently my husband, Steve, and I were asked to teach on grand-parenting for the mid-week services at our church, Willow Creek. On the coldest night that winter, we drove to Willow anticipating very little. Who would come out on this bleak midwinter night? After all, sub-zero temperatures typically translate to sub-zero response in Illinois. Plus, we're hardly grandparenting experts. But to our great surprise and delight, the room was packed, filled to standing-room-only capacity! And more, this crowd was ready and eager to talk about their grandparenting experiences—their joys, their challenges, and their heartbreaks.

We were blown away—completely shocked—by the response. This night was the beginning for us. We sensed God starting something new in this grandparenting season of our lives. And best of all, we discovered we're not alone. It seems God is starting a fresh movement, leading our generation of Christian grandparents into uncharted waters and calling us to a kind of intentional grand-parenting that is without precedent.

Together, we are asking God to show us how to bless our children's children and the children in generations yet unborn. We are asking God to impact our homes, extended families, churches, and the nations. We are asking Him to use our generation to draw people for many generations to himself.

A Mindset Makeover

For Steve and me, our thinking about these particular years of life has changed. I think of this change as before-and-after pictures.

Before, we were in denial about this time of life. Steve and I do not feel old and we flatter ourselves that we don't look that old—or at least we eagerly buy in whenever someone tells us so. We still have lots of energy and interest in life. Culture constantly bombards us with messages to work out, eat well, and learn to manage this season's physical challenges. And if this doesn't calm our anxiety, of course we could resort to Botox, facelifts, and retirement living in Florida to encourage the denial possibilities!

That was us before. The "after" us is more accepting that we may have only a limited time left for God to use us. We have a new sense of sweet urgency about our choices. We now fully realize what time it is!

Add to the "before" picture of denial another "before" picture. We used to operate with a subtle sense of entitlement. How could we not? Seniors are pummeled with cultural messages like

Take a vacation . . . you deserve a once-in-a-lifetime trip—or two.

Take your retirement . . . you've earned it.

Take the benefits . . . they're yours.

Take a break from responsibilities . . . enter a second childhood.

Take time for golf, shopping, and eating out . . . fill your remaining years with the good life.

We've begun to sense a danger here. While it's painful to acknowledge that the years ahead are fewer, we wonder if there's something to be gained in knowing what time it is. Reality brings focus. What do we really want these last precious years of our lives to be about?

This past Christmas brought some clarity on what is truly important to us. Our adult children were our guests, and it turned out to be a little challenging. I found myself meal planning and grocery shopping for the organic and non-allergenic foods they requested/needed. Medium-density tofu. Organic baby food in squeeze tubes. No dairy. No fish. Organic everything. It was inconvenient and out of my tried-and-true holiday cooking grid, not to mention expensive. But I didn't want it to be an issue at Christmas, especially since these family times are so rare.

I found focus and grounding in Steve's words, "It's not about us anymore, Valerie. This is the giving season of our lives."

What would make our sons' families feel welcome and comfortable in our home?

What would convey our love?

We heard the words of St. Francis from his prayer, "For it is in giving that we receive."[1]

In the end, we had a wonderful family Christmas, but with an awareness of how we could have blown it. "Giving season" meant that we, the senior adults, grew up a little bit more and decided not to fuss or complain, insisting on proper boundaries or other behaviors we had a "right" to expect.

It's so easy to lose focus and forget the point completely. When we step back from the cultural trends and remove ourselves from the "you-deserve-your-retirement" stream, we've found what we really want is very different from what we are being offered. Here it is: We want these years to be about our children and grandchildren. We want to highly invest in them spiritually and leave a lasting legacy of faith. When we focus, we realize these prime years in our lives offer unique opportunities to influence, encourage, and uplift. We want these years to be our giving years.

What follows are some of the gifts we're focusing on giving during this fleeting season of life.

The Gift of Flexibility

A few years back our oldest son had "the talk" with us. He and his wife wanted to have Christmas Day with their children at their own house and move our extended Bell family time to the day after Christmas. We weren't prepared for this, or really thrilled about it. We grieved our perceived loss of position in their lives and the long-established traditions we would no longer practice.

In retrospect, it worked. Two big meals became one brunch and a light supper. Sometimes they come late on Christmas Day and stay overnight, little ones sleeping in our beds and destroying our house—just the kind of chaos that means family to me. We've learned it is still Christmas, whether it's on December 25 or some other time. It's Christmas when we are celebrating together.

Flexibility is one of the best gifts grandparents can give their children and grandchildren.

The Gift of Presence

Some family studies indicate it is the grandmother who is the generational glue in families.[2] I have taken this to heart. But whether it's grandmother or grandfather, we shouldn't wait for anyone else to keep our family glued together. Our presence is reassuring.

There are many ways grandparents can be present for adult children in the throes of raising families. We can initiate the phoning and messaging—and not keep score if the favor is not returned to us. We can learn how to walk alongside their lives. Show interest. Ask questions. Be there. Even if it's via Skype. We can make it a regular part of the week to stay in touch. We grandparents can keep the distance closed between the generations.

Many times the gift of presence is connected to need. "Can you run the kids to Little League?" "Can you baby-sit?" We were thrilled when our youngest son finally married in his early thirties and announced he and his wife were going to be parents. We weren't prepared for the next ask: "Mom, after the baby comes, do you think you could come live with us for six months so we don't have to put a tiny baby in childcare?" Childcare for this precious and long-awaited child of theirs was their pressing need. I agreed I didn't want a tiny baby in childcare either. There was only one problem: They live in California; we are in Illinois.

I'm pretty sure I wouldn't have asked my mom for this kind of help. *Whose baby is this, anyway?* I wondered.

But we are living in different times. Times when we are all trying to get back on our economic feet after a devastating decade.

In the end, I became the "granny nanny" for three months. Steve traveled back and forth as he could. I kept my weekend speaking commitments from California. By working together, I had the privilege of getting to know my granddaughter early and well. On our daily stroll through the neighborhood, I learned she loved the outdoors. We had many "no cry" days together due to her convivial temperament. None of my own children were that adaptable. I was there to point this out to her parents. This little girl of theirs was special! And baby humor? She was and still is brimming with it.

The gift of presence is pronounced for 2.7 million American grandparents. They are raising their own grandchildren. And through divorce, drug abuse, and other unexpected problems, the ranks of grandparents raising grandchildren are increasing. "Whose child is this, anyway?" is a question they are answering through the sacrifice of their own lives. Hats off to such grandparents! May God bring to full realization the prayer of St. Francis in their lives, "For it is in giving that we receive."

The Gift of Joy, Celebration, and Belonging

We have friends who are "grandparents extraordinaire." Really, they are the best. When their grandchildren come to visit, they roll out an actual red carpet with accompanying banners that proclaim, "Welcome Jake! Welcome Anna!" What kid wouldn't love that?

I love the idea, and we have stolen it (although we have settled for a less complicated version), and it is received with as much love as it is given. When our grandsons visit, we greet them on the steps outside. We jump and clap. We spin around with our arms high in the air and shout, "The boys are here! The boys are here! Rowan and Rhys and Merrick and Griffin are here!" They come into our arms and house like proud, smiling conquerors of the world. Merrick is three and he particularly enjoys this ritual, going back and forth to his parents' car so he can be greeted many times. "Let's do that again!" he says. It never gets old.

The Gift of Spiritual Tools

Even toddlers can be taught how to know God. At our house this involves our bedtime sleepover ritual with grandchildren. Every night it is the same. Everyone cuddles up in Lovie's bed. (Lovie is my grandma name.) We read books together and laugh. Then each little hand is massaged . . . an "assagemay." Each finger then becomes a word of spiritual promise. Jesus says, "I (thumb) will (pointer finger) never (middle finger) leave (ring finger) you (pinkie)."

I tell each child, "You belong to us," and rehearse the names of all the family members who love them. We pray as I massage their heads. I tell them how much God loves them and that He has something special for them to do in the world. Soon they are asleep, surrounded by God's presence and the love of an entire extended family.

The Gift of God-Stories

We love to share our God-stories with our family. These are the stories of God's activity in our lives. Recently when our grandsons were eating with us, we told them how they almost did not come to be.

> Your mother and father were young college students when they started dating. Your father decided they were too young to get married, so he broke up with your mother. He told her they were too young to be serious, and he added, "We are never, ever getting back together." That whole winter and spring he was so sad and crabby. He really missed your mother. And we learned from your other grandparents that your mother was also miserable and spent a lot of time crying. Finally, toward the beginning of summer, your father said, "I think I've made a terrible mistake. I'm in love with Kailey. Dad, what should I do?"
>
> Gaago (Steve's grandpa name) told your dad he should start by crawling from our house to your mom's house to show her how sorry he was. Your dad tried desperately to get back together with your mom, but she was too angry at him. Finally, her dad told her she should give your dad another chance.
>
> And she did. (Phew!) A year later they got married and then had you guys—because God thought you four boys were an excellent idea.

Their eyes were big. They had never heard this God-story before. We ended by saying, "Before you were even born, God was looking out for you."

Recently we experienced a God-story when we were together. I was picking them up to go to Awana. The night was bitterly cold. I fumbled with their coats and boots, car seats, my keys, my purse, their Awana books. Feeling proud I had risen to the managing-kids'-bodies-and-car-seats challenge all by myself, I closed the passenger door, went around to the driver's side, and *Oh no!* the door was locked with my keys and my grandkids inside.

Yikes! In a voice that would scare any child, I coached our seven-year-old, Rowan, to unbuckle himself and crawl up to the driver's seat. He struggled to make out what I was saying. "Push the buttons on the armrest!" I kept yelling. It was dark in the car. He tried all the buttons, but nothing happened. Panic began to rise in me as I thought of how cold and afraid they would be if I couldn't get the door opened. I ran to the house and asked my daughter-in-law to call the police.

Utterly panic-stricken by now, I ran back to the car. And then I saw it. The door locks were up and out of their sockets, pointing to the ceiling! Rowan had managed to unlock the car—thank you, God!

When Rowan tells this shared God-story, he says he thought to himself, *I can do this!* He wasn't panicked at all. But he does have a sense of how God kept him calm and helped him rise to the occasion.

As we become more intentional in our spiritual grandparenting, we think about the generations to come—the children we will never hold, but who will have our eyes, or our sense of humor, or a natural openness for wonder and awe, or our stubbornness and willfulness. Though gone, we will touch them through the links of the chain of faith from our children to our grandchildren and to those who follow.

> I will open my mouth with a parable;
>> I will teach you lessons from the past—
> things we have heard and known,
>> things our ancestors have told us.
> We will not hide them from their descendants;
>> we will tell the next generation
>> the praiseworthy deeds of the Lord. . . .
> So the next generation would know them,
>> even the children yet to be born,
>> and they in turn would tell their children.

> Then they would put their trust in God
> and would not forget his deeds.
>
> Psalm 78:2–4, 6–7 TNIV

We are joining a growing movement of Christian grandparents who are experiencing a sweet urgency to be more spiritually intentional toward their grandchildren. And may the generations to come find the unshakable, unmovable trust in God they need for whatever lies ahead.

We know what time it is. It is giving season. May our children's children, and all those who follow, come to know and trust God through these gifts.

PART 2

GOD'S DESIGN

4

An Introduction to Grandparenting

Four Biblical Truths Every Grandparent Must Know

After speaking at a grandparent seminar, a discouraged grand-mother approached me and asked, "What do I have to offer my grandchildren? I don't have much money, and it's not very exciting to come to my house." If you have ever asked yourself some version of this question, then I want to remind you of an important truth that many Christian grandparents have forgotten: *Grandparents matter.*

Grandparents Matter

I've found that many grandparents underestimate their impact and undervalue their influence. It is as if the repeated cultural messages that minimize the importance of grandparents have been internalized and become the message grandparents repeat to themselves. Grandparents must not buy into the myth that they are unneeded, unwanted, or of little value. Grandparents have incredible value, and it is not in the gifts or experiences they provide grandchildren.

I want you to see a few reasons from Scripture why grandparents matter. This is not meant to be an exhaustive list, but a simple reminder that grandparents are important and have a lot to offer grandchildren that few people can match. If you are discouraged or have lost sight of the importance of grandparenting, I want you to read this section carefully to help restore the prominence God gives to grandparents in the lives of children and grandchildren.

Here are seven ways grandparents matter:

1. *Long-term relationship.* Friends come and go, but family remains. It is a true gift from God to have close family relationships. Like the father in Proverbs, a grandparent can say to a grandchild, "Give me your heart, and let your eyes observe my ways" (Proverbs 23:26). Other than parents, what relationship will your grandchild have that is lifelong and in close proximity to a Christlike person? For most young people that list is short, which enhances the incredible value of grandparents. There are few relationships in a person's life that will begin in the foundational years of childhood, continue through the identity-forming stage of adolescence, and be present into adulthood. That is significant, especially in a transient culture where families relocate geographically for work and where relationships are maintained through social media. The long-term nature of your relationship with a grandchild gives you the advantage over every other influencer short of parents. This was God's design to enable you to pass faith on to multiple generations. If you nurture the relationship with your grandchildren, you will have the opportunity to speak into their lives and shape their heart.

2. *Wisdom.* Wisdom is different from knowledge. Knowledge is the accumulation of information. Wisdom is the ability to apply that information to life situations. Wisdom includes moral skillfulness— the ability to make choices that are good and godly. Grandparents have two things working in

their favor: Wisdom is in short supply, and grandchildren need help making wise choices. If Proverbs is any indication, young people are prone to making foolish choices. Young people need help choosing the right friends, having the right affections, managing their money, and not being lazy. In Proverbs 4:7–8 young people are told, "Get wisdom, and whatever you get, get insight. Prize her highly." Grandparents are a source of wisdom to guide young people on paths of righteousness and to teach them that wisdom is only found in Christ (Proverbs 1:7).

3. *A good name.* What is one of the best gifts grandparents can pass on to future generations? According to the Bible it is a good name. A good name is more desirable than wealth (Proverbs 22:1) and better than the most expensive luxuries of life (Ecclesiastes 7:1). Why is a good name so valuable? It has to be slowly earned. It cannot be purchased. A good name takes a lifetime to build but can be lost in a moment. A good name makes it possible for a family to transfer portions of trust, credibility, and respect that have been earned over a lifetime to future generations. Trust is the foundation of all relationships and may open the door to opportunities that otherwise would not exist. Your grandchildren, and maybe even your children, may not understand the value of a good name. Remind them. Ultimately, viewed through the Gospel, the good name you give your family is the name of Christ, the name above all names. If you live your life for Christ, you will have a good name worth passing to future generations.

4. *Christlike character.* Little eyes are watching and little ears are listening to see if your life choices match your stated convictions. Your life is a powerful example; it is a daily sermon, and for the godly grandparent it becomes an ir- resistible invitation to future generations to imitate you as you imitate Christ. Every choice you make sends a message

to grandchildren about what you believe. In Deuteronomy 4:15, Moses instructs the community to "watch yourselves very carefully" so that children and grandchildren do not do what is evil, but follow God (Deuteronomy 4:9 and 25). Every word you speak reflects positively or negatively on Christ. In Colossians 4:6 Paul instructs the people of God to "Let your speech always be gracious, seasoned with salt." Why? In order to declare the mystery of Christ to others. In Titus 2, older generations are charged with teaching the younger generations Christlike character such as self-control (boys), and purity, kindness, and self-control (girls).

5. *Stability and strength.* Grandparents have weathered the storms of life and can use their experience to validate the truths of the Bible and remind grandchildren that God is sovereign and uses everything for good. Like Lois, you are the last line of defense and become a spiritual surrogate for grandchildren when assistance is needed (2 Timothy 1:5). Problems and discouragement are the inevitable norm of life. Not only do young people need to be trained to emotionally and spiritually grow in these moments, but they will need people to turn to in order to process and grieve the trials of life. It's easy to follow God when life is good. But what happens when disaster strikes? Children and grandchildren will either turn to God or turn from God. They will either grumble and get angry or find hope and joy in Christ. Crisis gives you the opportunity to teach grandchildren who Christ is, to be a stabilizing presence when death or divorce hits, and to step in as a spiritual surrogate.

6. *Joy in Jesus.* Why has God given you long life? I believe part of that answer is found in Paul's explanation to the Philippian church regarding why God had placed Paul in their life: "I know that I will remain and continue with you all, for your progress and joy in the faith, so that in me you may have

ample cause to glory in Christ Jesus" (Philippians 1:25–26). God has given you breath today to help your grandchildren glory in Christ and fight for joy in Jesus. Your grandchildren are on a quest for joy. They will find their delight in something, whether that is Jesus or a Jesus replacement. Grandparents help grandchildren look past difficult circumstances and "rejoice in the Lord always" (Philippians 4:4).

7. *The Gospel.* Grandparenting is not primarily about happy grandchildren or healthy relationships. Grandparenting is an artery that carries the Gospel to future generations. It's mainly about passing on a rich heritage in Christ to future generations. It's about teaching God's truth, giving testimony to the goodness and greatness of God, and living a life shaped by the Gospel. Grandparenting exists to deliver the Gospel to future generations, "For I delivered to you as of first importance what I also received: that Christ died for our sins in accordance with the Scriptures, that he was buried, that he was raised on the third day in accordance with the Scriptures" (1 Corinthians 15:3–4). Grandparenting matters because you have something to offer your grandchildren that the world can't.

Grandparents are difference-makers. You have much to offer that few people can replicate for your grandchildren. If you withhold that God-designed influence, your grandchildren have lost something of immeasurable worth. Don't listen to the voices telling you that you have little to offer or that your best days are behind you. Take your cues from the Bible. According to God, you matter.

God Designed Grandparenting

How would you complete the sentence "Grandparenting is for _____"? There are four options: yourself, children or grandchildren, the community, or God. Ultimately, how you answer this question will determine how you approach grandparenting.

Culture tells you that grandparenting is primarily about yourself. But we've already seen that this is not the correct focus. An equally problematic emphasis is a focus on the health and happiness of children or grandchildren.

You must have a settled conviction on this truth: *God designed grandparenting.* He created it. Grandparenting is God's idea. Colossians 1:16 states, "All things were created through him and for him." Grandparenting was created by God and for God. This is an important point for all Christian grandparents to understand because everything God creates, including grandparenting, He creates for a reason. If God created grandparenting, the natural question that arises is, why? God must have a purpose for it. What is grandparenting meant to accomplish?

God created grandparents to partner with parents to raise the next generation to treasure Christ. Grandparents and parents are teammates working toward the same biblical goals. We are fellow laborers created to point grandchildren to Christ, encouraging them to cultivate a God-centered life that passionately believes that to live is Christ and to die is gain.

Grandparents are the adjunct servant of the godly parent and the spiritual surrogate of the ungodly parent. What do I mean by that? God designed parents as the primary disciple-makers in a child's life, and grandparents as a secondary, but important, influence. If parents are raising children in the Lord, then grandparents support and encourage parents to fulfill the task God has given them and reinforce the work of the parent by investing directly into the spiritual life of a grandchild. If parents are not raising children in the Lord, then grandparents need to lovingly encourage parents to take seriously the responsibility God has given them, and if spiritual abdication occurs, the grandparent should seek to step into a more prominent disciple-making role in the life of a grandchild.

Godly parenting → Grandparents as Adjunct Servants
Ungodly parenting → Grandparents as Spiritual Surrogates

Parenting is difficult and becomes exponentially more difficult without the help or support of grandparents. God never intended parents to raise children alone. Instead, God gave families the gift of grandparents to share burdens, to distribute the weight of child-rearing, and as a means to provide multiple influences to raise children in the Lord.

Today's parents need help raising children, but unlike previous generations, they have the option to outsource portions of a grandparent's role to impersonal institutions or family surrogates such as preschools for baby-sitting, restaurants for Sunday dinner, movie theaters for a story, or parenting experts for child-rearing instruction. These grandparent replacements cannot usurp your role or fill your shoes, as they cannot provide wisdom, the love and affection of a grandparent, family traditions, or family history.

God created grandparents with a unique role and a specific function: Your job is to enthusiastically embrace God's design. When we reject the design, we reject the Designer. Grandparenting is not a take-it-or-leave-it cultural creation whose purpose and meaning change with each generation. God did not create grandparents as an unnecessary, optional appendage to the family. God created grandparents to play a crucial role in the spiritual development of grandchildren by linking arms with parents to work toward the same goals of raising future generations to know, love, and serve Jesus.

God-Centered Grandparenting

The Bible repeatedly teaches that *grandparenting is to be God-centered*. Psalm 145:3–4 states, "Great is the Lord, and greatly to be praised, and his greatness is unsearchable. One generation shall commend your works to another, and shall declare your mighty acts." Grandparents are instructed to declare God's greatness and mighty acts to future generations. Does that sound like you as a grandparent? Or have you centered grandparenting around something other than God and His mighty work in Christ?

God is to be the focal point, the reason for, and the all-consuming passion of grandparenting. Jesus summarized the law and the prophets with a phrase that boils down to "love God and love others (Matthew 22:37–40). We know this phrase as the great commandment, but it is also to be a great ambition of grandparenting. Do you grandparent in a way that helps your grandchildren grow in their love for God and love for others? If someone asked your grandchildren what was the most important thing to you in the world, what do you think your grandchildren would say? If a love for God in Christ Jesus does not top the list, then you have some reprioritizing to do.

What does it mean to be a God-centered grandparent in day-to-day life? It means your driving passion and priority is Jesus Christ; this is reflected in the decisions you make, the things you say, what you watch, how you spend your money, how you use your time, how you treat others, and the aroma of your life. A God-centered grandparent places Christ at the center of all these areas of life. Is Christ the foundation and the focal point around which all life centers? Grandchildren know what matters most to you, and if it is anything other than God, it communicates to grandchildren that their focus in life should be centered around something other than God.

Leaving a Heritage That Lasts

What one word would you choose to summarize the role of a grandparent? I've asked thousands of grandparents this question, and the most common answers include *love, encouragement, wisdom, support, family historian, intentionality*, and *storyteller*. These are good words and each represent an important portion of a grandparent's role. However, none of these words fully summarizes the role of a grandparent according to the Bible.

Every member of the family is given a clear, God-ordained role that is not interchangeable with other members of the family. Husbands are told to be the spiritual leader of the home and to lovingly serve their family (Ephesians 5:23). Wives are given the role of helper and are to willingly follow their husband's loving leadership (Genesis 2:18; Ephesians 5:22). Children are told to honor their parents through obedience (Exodus 20:12; Ephesians 6:1). If the Bible clearly defines the role of other family members, shouldn't it also define the role of a grandparent?

The role of a grandparent is best summarized by the word *heritage*. Grandparents are given the task of building a rich heritage in Christ that will outlive them. The word *heritage* suggests that grandparents have something valuable to give future generations. The author of Proverbs 13:22 states, "A good man leaves an inheritance to his children's children," which has financial and spiritual applications. Grandparents have received a spiritual heritage that God commissions them to pass on to future generations. There is nothing of greater value that you can give to your family than a love for Christ.

I can find no better biblical concept that fully describes the pattern and priorities for grandparents in Scripture than the word *heritage*. Moses (Deuteronomy 6:2) and the psalmist (Psalm 78) both are concerned with multigenerational faithfulness. The responsibilities that God explicitly gives grandparents such as teaching (Deuteronomy 4:9), testimony telling (Psalm 78:5), and character training (Titus 2:2–6) all exist for the greater purpose of passing on a heritage in Christ that lasts.

Take a moment to consider what type of heritage you are leaving your family. Are you laboring to leave a perishable heritage or an eternal one? Will your heritage be godly or ungodly? The Bible reminds us that a heritage can be lost, so we must give ourselves to passing on a faith that will last. A heritage in Christ must be received, so we must not assume about our grandchildren's salvation. A heritage other than Christ is of no eternal value, so we must not be seduced by the comforts of life. Every one of us will leave a heritage for our children and grandchildren. What will yours be?

Grandparenting matters to God and it should matter to you. God designed grandparents to be a key disciple-making influence with the central thrust of passing faith on to future generations. Grandparenting is to be God-centered, with a focus on loving God and loving others. Grandparents are given the task of building a rich heritage in Christ that lasts. These truths are the beginnings of a solid foundation for Christian grandparenting. They will help you reject the cultural messages about grandparenting, establish strong relationships in Christ, and pass on a rich heritage of faith to future generations.

Grand Chat

1. Have you ever felt discouraged as a grandparent? If so, in what way?

2. This chapter highlights seven ways grandparents matter: long-term relationship, wisdom, a good name, Christlike character, stability and strength, joy in Jesus, and the Gospel. What areas stand out to you as important? How have you experienced the importance of any of the seven areas?

3. What opportunities have you had to support your adult children as they raise and nurture the faith of your grandchildren?

4. Read Psalm 145:3–4. According to this passage, what responsibility do older generations have to younger generations? How have you applied this passage with your grandchildren?

5. If someone asked your grandchildren what is the most important thing in the world to you, what do you think your grandchildren would say?

5

Where Should I Start?

Applying Deuteronomy 4:9

When I teach on grandparenting, one of the common questions I'm asked is, "Where do I start?" That was the question I received from a group of grandparents who were motivated to pass their faith in Christ to future generations but were unsure where to focus their time and energy.

One grandfather from this group stated, "I want to be a good grandparent. I just don't know where to look or what to do; grandparenting wasn't modeled well for me." If you identify with this statement, you aren't alone. Over the years, many grandparents have communicated a similar sentiment to me.

I believe the best place to start is always with Scripture, and the most important thing to do is to understand the biblical role of a grandparent. Do you know what the Bible says about grandparenting? If someone asked you to help her understand the role of a grandparent, where would you direct her to in the Bible?

Grandparents Have a Biblical Role

The Bible has hundreds of references to grandparenting, but these references are often missed because the Bible uses phrases such as *children's children, son's son, father's father,* or *forefather* to speak of grandparenting. Here are a couple of examples. Take a moment to slowly read these six passages (emphasis added in each), and pay attention to the responsibilities that God gives grandparents.

- Deuteronomy 4:9. "Make them [God's commands] known to your children and your *children's children.*"
- Deuteronomy 6:2, 5–7. "Fear the Lord your God, you and your son and your *son's son,* by keeping all his statutes and his commandments, which I command you, all the days of your life, and that your days may be long. . . . You shall love the Lord your God with all your heart and with all your soul and with all your might. And these words that I command you today shall be on your heart. You shall teach them diligently to your children."
- Proverbs 17:6. "*Grandchildren* are the crown of the aged."
- Psalm 78:4–6. "Tell to the coming generation the glorious deeds of the Lord. . . . He established a testimony in Jacob and appointed a law in Israel, which he commanded our *fathers* to teach to their children, that the next generation might know them, the *children yet unborn.*"
- Psalm 92:12, 14–15. "The righteous flourish like the palm tree. . . . They still bear fruit in *old age*; they are ever full of sap and green, to declare that the Lord is upright; he is my rock, and there is no unrighteousness in him."
- 2 Timothy 1:5. "I am reminded of your sincere faith, a faith that dwelt first in your *grandmother* Lois."

Over the years I've heard all kinds of comments like, "How did I miss this?" "This is really exciting!" and "Tell me what I need to do. I'm ready to get started." Whatever your response, it is helpful to recognize that God has a lot of expectations for grandparents. God gives grandparents a significant role focused on helping future generations embrace the Gospel and treasure Christ. Even a quick glance at these passages reveals a major difference between God's role for grandparents and the culture's role for them. *God expects grandparents to be disciple-making, God-fearing, daily-impressing, grandchild-loving, testimony-telling, truth-teaching, fruit-bearing, and faith-filled individuals.* Let's look more closely at the first key passage of Scripture on grandparenting.

Deuteronomy 4:9

Deuteronomy 4:9 may be the most concise passage in the Bible on grandparenting: "Only take care, and keep your soul diligently, lest you forget the things that your eyes have seen, and lest they depart from your heart all the days of your life. Make them known to your children and your children's children." Let's look more closely at three critical aspects of grandparenting from Deuteronomy 4:9.

Grandparenting begins with the heart. Your walk with Christ is the most important aspect of grandparenting. The first step to being a grandparent has little to do with the right methods and everything to do with the right affections. Grandparenting begins with your own love for God. What you are passionate about impacts what your family becomes passionate about. Take a moment and think about what you love most in life. My guess is that many of your loves came from parents and grandparents. My love of fishing and the outdoors is a love passed down from my father and grandfather. My love for Jesus is a result of my parents' love for Jesus. Everything my parents did was guided by their first and greatest passion in life—Jesus—and that was appealing to me as a child.

Passion is infectious. What you treasure, your family likely will treasure. If you want your children and grandchildren to treasure Christ, then it must be obvious that you love Jesus with all your heart. It's the daily, mundane choices that transmit our values to future generations. You should pay close attention to three areas:

how you use your time, where you spend your money, and how you act. When a grandchild looks at how you spend your time, money, and actions, what conclusions will they make about what you love most?

I live in Minnesota where it is common for families to travel north to go to the lake for the weekend. What message does it send to a young person when week after week a grandchild sees their grandparent prioritize the cabin over church? Grandchildren are perceptive and quickly learn that entertainment is more important to the grandparent than gathering with a community of believers to worship God. A grandchild will begin to wonder, *If God or church isn't important for my grandparent, why should it be important for me?*

When asked, "Where do I start?" I take grandparents to Deuteronomy 4:9 and point out that it begins with the command, "Only care take and keep your soul diligently." How is your soul? Or said a different way, how is your love for Jesus? Have you been diligent to guard your heart and grow your love for Christ? Your grandchildren know what is most important to you and recognize if something other than Christ is the object of your greatest affections. The best thing you can do as a grandparent to pass on faith to future generations is love God with all your heart.

The Bible teaches that the real issues of life are spiritual and are matters of the heart. The word *heart* is used hundreds of times in the Bible and, depending on context, can refer to the mind, emotions, the will, sinful nature, or the inner person. The Bible tells us that God searches the heart (1 Samuel 16:7), and sin begins in the heart (Matthew 5:28).

Why is the heart so important? Because *what we do is a result of who we are.* The condition of your heart determines every aspect of your life, including what you do as a grandparent. That is why it is safe to say that grandparenting is a matter of the heart. Most writing on grandparenting focuses on methods. The idea is that if you aren't getting the right results, you must be doing the wrong things. But family literature that focuses on the external will never bring about lasting change. The starting place must be on your inner life—your thoughts, your motives, your values, and your beliefs.

Proverbs 4:23 states, "Above all else, guard your heart, for everything you do flows from it." Everything you do, including grandparenting, flows from your heart. You must pay careful attention to your heart because it is the fountainhead of grandparenting. If your heart is filled with evil, your life will be overrun by such passions. Our thoughts, words, and actions follow the heart. If the heart is allowed to be corrupt, one's life will be as well.

Moralists forget the heart and focus attention on behavior. Adopting new methods, altering environment, removing privileges, or virtue-based education without heart change will be in vain. It will lead to self-righteousness or rebellion. Unless the heart is made right with God, the very best schemes of life fail to cause any lasting life transformation.

There are three ways to guard your heart:

1. *Keep it full.* Our heart needs to be filled daily with the Word of God. An empty heart becomes the servant of another love, filled with the wrong concerns and prone to carelessness. We are to "meditate on it [God's Word] day and night, so that you may be careful to do according to all that is written in it" (Joshua 1:8). Psalm 1:2–3 states that the person who meditates on God's Word will yield fruit, and all that he does will prosper. Fruitful grandparenting is an outcome of faithfully filling up on God's Word.

2. *Keep it pure.* By nature, our heart is desperately wicked (Jeremiah 17:9–10). Purity does not naturally flow from it. Due to our bent toward sin, we still possess a capacity for evil. Thus, we must be mindful of what goes into our heart so as not to throw fuel on our sinful passions. What we watch and listen to matters, as a polluted fountain leads to muddied

living and does not result in training young people to live a godly life. Philippians 4:8 reminds us, "Whatever is true, whatever is honorable, whatever is just, whatever is pure, whatever is lovely, whatever is commendable . . . think about these things." Take a moment and assess what you are letting into your heart, according to the list provided in Philippians 4:8. Are there changes that you need to make?

3. *Keep it peaceful.* Many of us carry emotional burdens that God doesn't intend for us to bear. God wants us to diligently pay attention to what we think about, but also to what we feel. Paul tells us, "Let the peace of Christ rule in your hearts" (Colossians 3:15). Our hearts are to be peaceful places, yet for many individuals the inner self is a violent storm of churning emotions and fearful feelings. One of the common commands in the Bible is to "fear not." That is a reminder that many anxious hearts need to hear and heed today. Anxiety is always a result of trying to control the future, which is something only God can do. The Bible commands us to trust in the Lord, which is God's answer for anxious hearts. Peace is a by-product of trust. If you struggle with anxiety, God's antidote is to release control and trust in His sovereignty.

What is the condition of your heart? How well are you guarding it? What a grandparent *does* is important, but who a grandparent *is* is all-important.

A Grand Vision of Our Great God

Grandparenting is driven by a grand vision of God. Moses has a warning for every grandparent: "Lest you forget the things that your eyes have seen, and lest they depart from your heart all the days of your life" (Deuteronomy 4:9). The grandparent who loses sight of a grand God will give allegiance to another god. This passage reminds us that there are men and women of faith who have started well but finished poorly. Have you known anyone whose love for the Lord faded toward the end of life? Have you known someone whose passion for God only lasted for a portion of her life? Let us not presume lifelong faithfulness to God and become complacent in our walk with Christ.

God sets a lofty goal for grandparents: *Love the Lord with all your heart for all your days.* Loving God for all one's days is not easy. Maintaining a white-hot passion for God takes work. I want you to consider two examples from the Bible, one positive and one negative.

A positive example is Caleb, who "was forty years old when Moses the servant of the Lord sent me. . . . I wholly followed the Lord my God. . . . And now, behold, I am this day eighty-five years old. I am still as strong today as I was in the day that Moses sent me" (Joshua 14:7–8, 10–11). Caleb's obedience and love for God remained strong all his days and were passed down to future generations. If you want to be inspired, read Joshua 15:13–14, where it describes Caleb as a man of faith who became a giant slayer. It's worth noting that Caleb's nephew Othniel helped Caleb slay giants, and it is no coincidence that Othniel became the first judge in the book of Judges (Joshua 15:16–19; Judges 3:9–11). Do not miss the impact of lifelong faith on future generations. A life of radical faith is appealing. A lifetime of faith invites those behind you to follow in your footsteps.

A negative example is Demas, who is mentioned three times in the New Testament by Paul. He is the sad example of someone who departed from the faith, as Moses described in Deuteronomy 4:9. At the beginning of Paul's ministry he refers to Demas as a "fellow worker" who sent his greetings to the Colossian church (Philemon 1:24; Colossians 4:14). Demas was a key ministry associate of Paul and was well known by numerous churches, but sadly is remembered for his failure to love God all his days. In 2 Timothy 4:10 Paul states, "For Demas, in love with this present world, has deserted me and gone to Thessalonica." We don't know much about Demas, but we can see his faith trajectory. Demas loved the world more than Christ and walked away.

Caleb or Demas. Faithful for life or lover of the world. You will be one or the other. And wherever you land, it will have an impact on your grandchildren's faith. Will it be said of you that you loved God all your days, or loved this present world more?

What leads to a heart that grows cold and begins to love the wrong things? In Deuteronomy 4:9 Moses tells us that it is forgetting the things your eyes have seen—the work and words of God fail to penetrate and transform the heart.

If the danger is forgetting, then the remedy is remembrance. We must constantly be reminded of the glory of God and the supremacy of Christ. Do everything you can to ensure that your vision of God is great. If your God is small, you will find a God substitute that appears larger than life. This is what happened to Demas, and it can happen to us. We must guard against allowing ourselves to imagine that a God who was once majestic has become mundane, who once inspired awe is now ordinary—who was once *the* priority now is *a* priority.

One of the best things you can do as a grandparent is to fuel your understanding of who God is. How do you do that? Work diligently to delight in the greatness and goodness of God as seen in Scripture. Pray that God would set your heart ablaze to treasure Christ and to see His beauty. The result is a vision of God who is great, not small. God is seen as awesome and majestic, mysterious and mighty, and this biblical vision of God demands our worship. His greatness cannot be fathomed and the depths of His character cannot be measured. His love is amazing; hope is free, joy unlimited, and peace beyond comprehension. He is the God who sought us while we were yet sinners, holds the world in His hands, knows every hair on our head, controls the wind and the waves, spoke the world into existence, is sovereign over all, places kings on thrones, gives and takes life, is without beginning or end, and has no equal.

When God is big, everything else in life pales in comparison. When God is small, suddenly other things become more appealing. Exotic vacations, star athletes, and the luxuries of life become great and glorious when God is not. Grandparent, do not forget the glorious God your eyes have seen so that like Caleb, you continue to fight the good fight of the faith *all* your days.

Grandparents are teachers. Moses states, "Teach them [God's commands] to your children and your children's children." God wants to see the pattern of rebellion broken and faithfulness established, and the method God introduces to build lifelong faith is family discipleship from older generations to younger generations, centered on teaching God's truth.

In a day and age when it is popular to minimize teaching, it's good to remember that God places a high value on verbal instruction from older to younger generations. You've probably heard someone say, "More is caught than taught," and utilize this statement as justification to limit instruction. What I see the Bible teaching is that truth is caught *and* taught. The principle for grandparents to remember: *Christlike example and Bible-based teaching are both important.*

What are grandparents to teach grandchildren? Grandparents are to teach obedience to God's commands. In the context of Deuteronomy 4 we are given very specific instructions regarding the content of teaching. Deuteronomy 4:5 states, "I have taught you statutes and rules," and it is these commands that the older generation are to teach the younger. In Deuteronomy 5 Moses summoned all Israel and introduced the Ten Commandments, which are God's commands condensed, to be taught to future generations. To teach grandchildren well, there are three encouragements to consider:

- *Avoid moralism.* It is easy for teaching to become a list of do's and don'ts that focus on good vs. bad behavior. True and lasting behavior change comes when the heart is transformed. Thus, teaching must focus on the heart rather than behavior. For example, when a grandchild steals, the heart issue is greed. If a grandchild does not obey a parent, the heart issue is rebellion.

- *Focus on passion for God and compassion for others.* Jesus summarized the Ten Commandments as love God (the first four commandments) and love others (the last six commandments) in Luke 10:27. Ultimately, our desire is to see grandchildren treasure Christ.

- *Address relativism.* Your grandchild is growing up in a culture that believes right and wrong are determined by the individual, not by God as defined in the Bible. If your grandchild has embraced relativism to any degree, God's commands will have no effect on him or her. Before God's commands will be received, you must convince your grandchild that God determines what is right and wrong.

Grandparents have been given the responsibility of teaching future generations to obey God's commands. We will explore this in greater depth when we examine Psalm 78, but for now I will point out that this sounds similar to the Great Commission from Matthew 28:18–20. Jesus instructs His followers to go and make disciples by teaching others to obey all that God has commanded, which we will explore in the context of grandparenting.

Grandparenting begins with the heart, is driven by a grand vision for God, and is centered on teaching grandchildren to obey God. May we all be like Caleb, who was faithful for life and impacted the faith of future generations.

Grand Chat

1. Read the following verses and discuss the responsibilities God gives to grandparents and how they apply in each passage:

a. Deuteronomy 4:9

b. Deuteronomy 6:2–9

c. Proverbs 17:6

d. Psalm 78:4–8

e. Psalm 92:12–15

f. 2 Timothy 1:5

2. When a grandchild observes how you spend your time, money, and energy, what conclusions will they make about what you love most?

3. Read the following passages and discuss the state of your heart in each area:

a. Your daily devotions: Joshua 1:8

b. What you allow into your mind: Philippians 4:8

c. Your emotional state: Colossians 3:15

4. What can we learn from the examples of Caleb and Demas? Have you known any individuals who are like Caleb and exhibit lifelong faith, or Demas, who became a lover of the world?

5. In what ways have you been a teacher to your grandchildren?

6

What Is the Role of a Grandparent?

Grandparenting Is Discipleship

What is God's purpose for the family? The family was created by God to make disciples of Jesus Christ and equip children to serve God with their life. The family exists to steward the mission of God from one generation to the next. Matthew 28:18–20 summarizes God's mission for all believers, including grandparents: "Go therefore and make disciples of all nations." A grandparent's mission is to make disciples of Jesus Christ, who love God and love others and teach future generations to do the same. Rob Rienow states it this way:

> He [God] created your family to be a spiritual transformation center. It is the primary environment where faith and character are formed and shaped. God made your family so that you would help each other to love him more. You are together so that you might help each other discover Christ together, grow in him together, and together make a difference in the world for him.[1]

What are your grandparenting priorities? When your grand-children become adults, what do you want most for them? Over the years I've heard all kinds of answers to this question, but some common answers include: raising independent children; having happy and healthy grandchildren, a well-educated family, successful children; developing strong relationships, having fun, and creating memories; providing family support; and loving and serving Jesus.

When provided with this list, almost every Christian grandparent will identify grandchildren who love and serve Jesus as the top priority. However, when I began to dig deeper into grandparenting practices, I found that the day-to-day actions of many grandparents reflected a different priority. From the perspective of the Bible, our priority is to raise children and grandchildren who love the Lord, want to serve Him, and desire to please Him. The world needs more people who love Jesus and will bring the Gospel to the nations. That's why God gave you children and grandchildren. God gave grandparents the mission of making disciples of future generations, so let's explore what this means.

What Is Discipleship?

Discipleship is a term used to summarize the entire process of coming to faith and growing in spiritual maturity as a follower of Christ. Discipleship begins when rebel sinners place believing faith in the person and work of Jesus (Romans 10:9). After coming to faith in Jesus, the task of discipleship focuses on helping a believer grow in spiritual maturity as a follower of Christ. Discipleship is an invitation to orient our affections and desires to God's. It is the work of continually re-forming our thinking and habits to align with God's. Discipleship is the process by which an individual who has received new life takes on the character of Jesus and commits to living in obedience to God's commands.

Jesus defined *discipleship* in two words: "*Follow me.*" A disciple is a learner whose goal is to become like Jesus. When we follow

Jesus, it is for the purpose of becoming like Him in character and helping others do the same. A disciple is transformed by the power of God from the inside out and, as a result, his or her behavior becomes Christlike. A disciple is expected to replicate his or her teacher's way of life. Thus, our primary goal in discipleship is imitating Christ.[2] When Paul exhorts, "Imitate me as I imitate Christ" (1 Corinthians 11:1 GW), it is an invitation to be His disciple.

Bill Hull, author of *The Complete Book of Discipleship*, states, "Discipleship ranks as God's top priority because Jesus practiced it and commanded us to do it."[3] If discipleship is God's top priority, it should also be a grandparent's top priority. Let's take a quick look at Matthew 28:18–20 to learn how discipleship applies to grandparenting.

> And Jesus came and said to them, "All authority in heaven and on earth has been given to me. Go therefore and make disciples of all nations, baptizing them in the name of the Father and of the Son and of the Holy Spirit, teaching them to observe all that I have commanded you. And behold, I am with you always, to the end of the age."

According to Matthew 28:19–20, disciple-making includes three elements:

1. *Belief.* The first step in making disciples of your children and grandchildren is evangelism and is emphasized in the Great Commission by the statement that tells us to baptize them. Baptism is the public profession of faith in Jesus, and it is to be the first step for a new Christian. In Scripture, new belief is closely connected to baptism. For example, Acts 8:12 states, "they believed . . . and . . . were baptized." It is critical for grandparents to regularly share the Gospel with children and grandchildren and remind them of the good news of Jesus' death and resurrection. When a grandchild professes

faith in Christ and shows the signs of a regenerate heart, the next step is to encourage a grandchild to be baptized.

2. *Growth.* Once God has drawn a grandchild to himself and the grandchild has responded in faith, the next step is becoming more Christlike in character. Jesus commands us to teach them to obey, which is the central aspect of discipleship. Grandparents are to teach Gospel truths and, like the father in Proverbs, encourage young people to apply God's truth to life (Proverbs 1:8–9). Obedience to God is an essential element of discipleship.

3. *Going.* Once a follower of Jesus is trained, he or she is to be sent to share the Gospel and help others grow in faith. Jesus commands us to "go" and repeat the process with others, so a key element of discipleship is training children and grandchildren to make disciples of others. Grandchildren are to be equipped to use their gifts, skills, and passions to introduce others to Christ and help them mature in faith. Your grandchildren should be given a vision to reach their family, neighbors, and the nations for Christ.

In order to accomplish the task that God has given grandparents, three skills can be developed to correlate to each phase of discipleship. Grandparents should learn to share the Gospel with their family (to encourage belief in Jesus), teach the Bible to children and grandchildren (to cultivate growth in Christ), and equip grandchildren to serve (to launch them into the world). We will explore these in greater depth in chapters 10 and 11, but for now let's explore family discipleship based on Deuteronomy 6.

Multigenerational Family Discipleship

Deuteronomy 6 describes your dual discipleship role with children and grandchildren. This family discipleship passage describes *who* you are to disciple, *what* goal you are aiming for, and *how* you are to go about making disciples of your family. Let's explore each briefly.

If you are unfamiliar with Deuteronomy 6, I want to encourage you to take a moment and read it. The most common place to begin reading is Deuteronomy 6:4–9, but if we start reading there, we miss the broader context of this passage and incorrectly interpret this passage as exclusively written to parents.

Based on the context of Deuteronomy 6, the commands of this passage apply to grandparents as well. Moses, in Deuteronomy 6:2, states the commands of God are for "you and your son and your son's son." Notice the terms "son" and "son's son." This multi-generational reference is not a throwaway statement but a call to action to disciple your children and grandchildren. The commands of Deuteronomy 6 are written for grandparents as well as parents.

Disciple the Disciple-Makers

Grandparenting, in part, is the task of discipling the disciple-makers. Grandparenting is more than what you do directly with your grandchildren. A key discipleship principle from the Bible for our family: *Parents are primary and grandparents are secondary disciple-makers.*

The Bible clearly places the responsibility on parents to raise children in Christ by teaching children the truths of the Bible and by modeling a life that is worthy of imitation. The most powerful impact on the faith of children is parents who practice what they preach. Parents who live out their faith present a compelling and persuasive example in front of young people that is contagious. Grandparents must be careful not to usurp a role that God has given parents, but should support parents to raise their children in the Lord (Ephesians 6:4).

Sociologist Christian Smith states, "No other conceivable casual influence . . . comes even remotely close to matching the influence of parents on the religious faith and practices of youth."[4] Thus, it is strategic to do everything possible to encourage adult children to grow spiritually and raise their children to love Jesus. You are indirectly discipling your grandchildren when you encourage and equip your adult children to faithfully raise their children in the Lord.

Paul and Diana Miller, authors of *A Guide to Great Grandparenting*, state, "Our first responsible role as grandparents is to coach our adult children as they learn how to parent."[5] Every investment you make in your children is an investment you make in your grandchildren. Every time you help your adult child grow spiritually, develop a stronger marriage, or grow as a parent, you are benefitting your grandchild. God has given you a dual role that is to focus on your children and children's children.

One of the most impactful things a grandparent can do is to invest in the spiritual life of adult children and encourage parents to prioritize the faith development of children. If parents lack the passion or do not prioritize faith in Christ, then grandparents have an opportunity to invest spiritually in a more significant manner.

When do you complete the task of discipleship as described in Deuteronomy 6? I do not see any indication from the Bible that this task ever stops. It simply changes as a child ages. In God's economy, the spiritual work of a parent is never done. It takes different shapes through different stages of life, but it never fully goes away. Thus, grandparenting isn't just about grandchildren. Grandparenting is concerned with children as much as it is grandchildren. I want you to consider the investment you make relationally, spiritually, and emotionally in your adult children vs. your grandchildren. How much time and energy is devoted to each generation? Have you reduced grandparenting to what you do with grandchildren, or do you have a broader role as reflected in the Bible?

Five Phases of Discipling Children

God has given you the task of making disciples of your family. That goal never changes. Children never outgrow their need for Jesus or to continue maturing in Christ. As long as you have breath, you have a role encouraging children to know Christ and grow in Him. Most Christians would agree with that statement; however, the big question is how do you do that when a child becomes an adult? I've found it helpful to view parenting in five phases.[6]

- *Caregiver*: The parent cares for all the needs of a child such as food, clothes, and hygiene. Season of life: infant and pre-school. Biblical example: "Behold, children are a gift of the Lord" (Psalm 127:3 NASB).
- *Commander*: The parent controls every area of the child's life and corrects the child to encourage holiness in Christ. Season of life: Grade school. Biblical example: "Children, obey your parents in the Lord" (Ephesians 6:1).
- *Coach*: The parent delegates decision-making as a child matures, models Christlike living, and releases responsibility. Season of life: Adolescence. Biblical example: "Imitate me as I imitate Christ" (1 Corinthians 11:1 GW).
- *Counselor*: The parent offers biblical guidance to navigate life choices and challenges. Season of life: Early adulthood. Biblical example: "Without counsel plans fail, but with many advisors they succeed" (Proverbs 15:22).
- *Consultant*: The parent provides godly wisdom from a lifetime of experience and mentors adult children to make disciples of their children. Season of life: Adulthood. Biblical example: "Be wise, my son, and bring joy to my heart" (Proverbs 27:11 NIV).

These phases can be a useful guideline when you are trying to discern how to interact with your adult child. Many individuals make the mistake of parenting an adult child as if they were a younger child. I guarantee that is one way a parent will exasperate a child (Ephesians 6:4). Every parent experiences the day when their influence changes from direct to indirect and a child desires greater independence. Each phase of parenting has its challenges, but the later phases can be especially difficult because they require letting go.

My friend Larry Fowler talks about the difference between control and influence in parent-child interaction. We know that parent involvement looks different as children age, yet sometimes we struggle to understand exactly how. When a child is young, control is high. Parents control what a child eats, when a child sleeps, and who the child associates with. As the child ages, control is slowly released and parental involvement shifts to influencing decisions, speaking into relationships, and guiding life direction.

Problems surface when parents give a young child too much autonomy to make decisions and share authority with children. Problems also surface when parents seek to control the decisions of an adult child and maintain authority over their life. Grandparents who attempt to control an adult child's decision or direction will either experience an unhealthy dependence from an adult child or find themselves in a battle for authority in which an adult child will reject the advice or retreat from the relationship.

Control   Influence

If your child has ever rejected your attempt to speak into her life, evaluate your method. Were you operating more as a commander and coach or a counselor and consultant? Your goal is to learn to use the right method for the moment. Methods matter because if you try to instruct an adult child by lecturing or attempt to maintain control, it probably won't be received well. More than likely it will result in resistance and possibly resentment.

I've had countless young parents tell me they wish they had a mentor who is willing to invest in them. They want someone who will listen, love, and guide them. Do you know who God created to be that mentor? You. Here are some ideas to help you do that:

- *Make yourself available.* Let your adult child know that they are a priority and you are available. We experienced this blessing from my wife's dad during a difficult day. While Jen was driving, a belt in the engine of our minivan broke and she was stranded on the side of the road. She couldn't get ahold of me (I was at the dentist), so she called her dad, who met her at the mechanic and discussed what needed to be done to the van. Then he took her out for dinner, where Jen discussed with Dan whether or not we should keep our minivan. Dan was able to speak into our lives simply because he made himself available, and we listened to his advice.

- *Become an askable parent.* There are two phrases an adult child will like to hear from you: "Feel free to call" (make sure you answer) and "Let me know how I can help." When your child has a question or needs help, you want to be one of the first people they turn to. My dad offered to help me if I needed assistance with my boat, so I called to ask him to help me change the ball bearings, and we had a wonderful afternoon together.

- *Regularly call with no agenda and no strings attached.* It is often during the normal, everyday conversations when your adult child will casually bring up a topic they have been thinking about and ask for your advice. If your adult child is busy and can't have a long conversation, don't be discouraged. Simply take what they are able to give and commit to regularly communicating with them.

- *Ask how you can pray for them.* The act of asking shows your adult child that you care, which may encourage him to share the joys and challenges he is facing and lead to opportunities for you to lovingly care for and guide him.

Your job is to help your adult children mature in faith so they can help their children do the same. One of my favorite ways to do this is to provide Bible-based, Christ-centered books to parents. Make it a priority to help your children build a library of good books that will help them be faithful parents. Here are a couple of my go-to books for parents:

- Learning to parent: *Visionary Parenting* by Rob Rienow
- Discipline: *Shepherding a Child's Heart* by Tedd Tripp
- Family Worship: *Family Worship* by Donald Whitney
- Worshiping as a family at church: *Parenting in the Pew* by Robbie Castleman
- Sex, purity, and marriage: *Preparing Children for Marriage* by Josh Mulvihill
- Biblical worldview: *What Does the Bible Say About That?* by Kevin Swanson
- Family Devotions: *Long Story Short* and *Old Story New* by Marty Machowski

Discipling Grandchildren

Grandparents are also called to disciple their grandchildren. If the commands of God are for your grandchildren, that implies that you share in the joy of teaching them diligently and talking about them regularly (Deuteronomy 6:7). Theologian Roy B. Zuck writes, "Teaching the young God's ways is a responsibility assigned not only to parents, but also to grandparents."[7] To suggest that it is only a parent's job to teach a child to obey the commands of the Lord fails to take into account passages of Scripture such as Deuteronomy 4:9 and 6:2. According to the Bible, grandparents share in the joy of imparting the truth of God to the next generation.

What are grandparents to teach grandchildren? Grandparents are to instruct their grandchildren to walk obediently before the

Lord and fear Him all the days of their lives (Deuteronomy 4:10; 14). What does it mean to fear God? Let's allow the Bible to answer this question. Psalm 33:8 states, "Let all the earth fear the Lord; let all the inhabitants of the world stand in awe of him!" To fear God is to stand in awe of His power, love, justice, wisdom, and especially the life, death, and resurrection of Jesus. To fear God is to see His greatness and respond in adoration, and that results in obedience.

Every grandchild is hard-wired to stand in awe of something or someone. Those who do not fear God stand in awe of worldly success, beauty, and power. They are going to be impressed by God or the things of this world. God has placed you in the life of your grandchildren to do everything you can to help them be captivated by God rather than this world.

Grandchildren who do not fear God live as if the world is the ultimate threat and joy to be concerned with. When your grandchild believes the world is the primary threat and joy, she gives it undeserved power over her passions and priorities. The biblical picture is different. The Bible tells us to fear God, not man. Romans 3 states that our primary sin is to have no fear of God at all. Sinful people have every reason to fear God's judgment (Hebrews 10:31). Fearing God is good because it is a catalyst for repentance and obedience. A healthy fear reminds a young person to take their eyes off the temporal and look to the eternal.

The Bible speaks about fearing God as a positive thing. Moses chose leaders because they feared God and wouldn't take bribes (Exodus 18:21). Proverbs tells young people that fear of the Lord is the beginning of wisdom (Proverbs 1:7). Paul tells us to work toward holiness because we fear God (2 Corinthians 7:1). Jesus told us to fear God who can destroy body and soul in hell (Matthew 10:28). The psalmist states, "Come, O children, listen to me; I will teach you the fear of the Lord" (Psalm 34:11). Like the psalmist, God is calling you to teach your grandchildren the fear of the Lord.

What does Deuteronomy 6 grandparenting look like? Here are two examples to give you a vision of how that might appear in your life. Both of these stories are shared from grandchildren who are reflecting on the spiritual influence their grandparents had on them.

Grandpa Faris was a retired pastor who lived near our home and who served as a ruling elder in a church planting effort in which we participated. I learned what grief is from him in my grandmother's death when I was young. In my high school years, we would meet at the local country golf course after I got off work and we'd play a quick nine holes. Sometimes that happened six days a week. Some people thought it was just a glorified cow pasture; but it was like green pastures beside still waters to me with Grandpa Faris there. He taught me about contentment, joy, God's covenant, and seeing the grace of God illustrated all around us in creation. He sat at our table each Saturday evening, and through the laughter and the stories and the singing, his love for the Lord gave me a very settled sense that we can indeed trust our sovereign Lord.[8]

Another grandchild shares the influence of his grandfather on him.

I'd spend more time with my maternal grandfather in my college years. But, even in high school, he took me to a lot of basketball and football games. As an elder in the church that sent our family into church planting, his wisdom in leadership and shepherding oozed out of his pores. He exercised hospitality with my grandmother like no other elder I've ever seen. He always had at least one young man into whom he was intentionally investing his life. He'd often greet me with "How are you, young man?" and an outstretched hand. He had the knack of making me feel like I belonged with the grown-ups. His political wisdom as a public servant was passed down over the dinner table and on car rides; you learned to love your community while with him.[9]

That is Deuteronomy 6 grandparenting. I want you to notice the amount of time these grandfathers invested in their grandsons. That is a key ingredient to passing faith to future generations. I also want you to notice the intentionality of these grandfathers. There wasn't anything extraordinary about what they did. They played golf, ate meals together, attended sporting events, and rode in the car together. These life moments became the vehicle to talk about Christ and pass on biblical wisdom. The life moments may look different for you, but the outcome can be the same. For these grandparents, passing on their faith wasn't one more thing they did, it was part of their everyday life. You can do the same thing.

Grand Chat

1. When your grandchild becomes an adult, what do you want most for him or her?

2. In your own words, how does the Bible summarize discipleship, and how does that apply to grandparenting? (See Matthew 28:18–20 and Deuteronomy 6:2–9).

3. What is your reaction to the following statement? "The world needs more people who love Jesus and will bring the gospel to the nations. That's why God gave you children and grandchildren." How does this statement impact your thinking for your family?

4. In what ways do you intentionally disciple your children and grandchildren?

5. Share an example of a time your adult child received or rejected your attempt to speak into his or her life. What did you learn from that experience?

7

God's Vision for Your Family from Psalm 78

How to Be an Intentional Grandparent

Linda, a grandmother of seven, with excitement in her voice, asked me, "There has been no pioneer in my life to model intentionality for me. Would you help me become more intentional? I don't want to miss the everyday opportunities with my family."

Everyday opportunities exist for each of us. Do you want to be intentional and capitalize on opportunities as they arise? Gospel-intentionality is possible when three things are understood:

1. **You have a weighty responsibility.** God has given you an incredible responsibility by entrusting you with children and grandchildren. It is a calling that deserves the best of your time and energy. Grandparents often struggle to discuss Christian matters with their family. Many grandparents are operating on a day-to-day basis and do not have a big-picture plan to spiritually invest in children and grandchildren. This results in missed opportunities and minimized impact.

2. **Many grandparents lack intentionality.** In general, Christian grandparents do not have a plan for the spiritual development of their family, often do not consider it a priority, and have little to no training in how to nurture their family's faith. Many Christian grandparents rely on others to introduce their grandchildren to Christ and grow them in their faith. I've found that most Christian grandparents desire to provide substantial training to children and grandchildren but are often unprepared to do so.

I realize this is a strong statement to make, but years of study and countless conversations with grandparents reveal this is the norm, not the exception. Here are two examples from in-depth conversations I've had with Christian grandparents: "Until you called, I really hadn't given much thought about what we were actively doing in depth with the grandkids." A different grandparent said, "I'm not sure I have a real good vision for that."

We need to think deeply about God's vision for our family and the goals He has for our children and grandchildren, and commit to God's methods to raise future generations to treasure Christ.

3 **You need clarity.** Gospel-intentionality is only possible when we have clarity of purpose. By definition, *intentionality is action by design*. Applied to family, intentionality is the pre-planned implementation of God's instruction. Intentionality involves an understanding of desired outcomes and an awareness to look for opportunities toward that end. It means eating meals, attending an athletic event, or baby-sitting with an eye toward a greater goal. The purpose of grandparenting is not happy grandchildren; rather, its aim is holy grandchildren.

I hope this chapter helps you become an intentional grandparent. Like Linda, you may not have had intentionality modeled for you. Thankfully, we have the Bible for that purpose. Psalm 78 is the most comprehensive passage in the Bible on grandparenting. It summarizes the role and the responsibility God has given older generations with future generations, speaks to the end goal of grandparenting, communicates discipleship methods, and contains a somber warning of failed family discipleship for all to heed. A clear understanding of Psalm 78 will aid your ability to be intentional and impact future generations with the love and truth of Christ.

Preparing Your Heart

Read Psalm 78

The first thing you need to do is read Psalm 78 and become familiar with the passage. Even if you have read the passage before, I encourage you to read it again. Try reading it now and then return to this book. You may want to make Psalm 78 your daily devotional.

Ask God to give you eyes to see and ears to hear

Next, ask God to help you understand what is being communicated in this passage. The Spirit of God works through the Word of God to change our heart. Pray that God would work in your heart to grasp the meaning and application of Psalm 78.

Adjust your ways to God's ways

Finally, acknowledge that God's ways are the best ways and be willing to change how you grandparent to align with Psalm 78. My hope is that our study of Psalm 78 does one of two things: provides confidence and affirms that you are headed in the right direction, or provides clarity and encourages you to adjust your ways. Psalm 78 reminds us that God has called grandparents to a very specific task and has given grandparents specific methods to accomplish a specific goal.

Understanding God's Vision for Your Family

Psalm 78 and Grandparenting

One of the first priorities in studying Psalm 78 is to determine if it applies to grandparents or if this passage speaks exclusively to parents. I believe it applies to grandparents for two reasons. First, in Psalm 78:5 we are told that a command was given to "our fathers." The word *fathers* is one of the Bible's ways of speaking about grandparents. In this context it means "forefathers" or "grandfathers." The second, and most convincing proof for me, is the multigenerational reference made in verses 5 and 6 to "children," "the next generation," and "children yet unborn." Clearly, the psalmist isn't just thinking mono-generationally. He has a multigenerational picture that extends beyond a single generation. While Psalm 78 unquestionably applies to parenting, it also applies to grandparenting.

A somber warning

Psalm 78 is a somber passage to read. It was written as a warning to motivate you to action. This is a historical psalm that recounts the repeated disobedience of the Israelites from the time of slavery in Egypt to the reign of King David. Psalm 78 is called a parable (v. 2), which means it's meant to teach a spiritual truth. The psalm encourages parents and grandparents to look at the failed example of others in history and imagine what might happen if we follow the same path with our family.

A quick scan of Psalm 78, starting in verse 9, describes what happens when older generations do not pass on faith in God to younger generations.

- They "forgot his works and the wonders that he had shown them" (v. 11).
- "They sinned still more against him" (v. 17).
- "They did not believe in God" (v. 22).
- "Their heart was not steadfast toward him" (v. 37).
- "They tested God again and again" (v. 41).
- "They turned away and acted treacherously" (v. 57).

Psalm 78:8 states, "That they should not be like their fathers, a stubborn and rebellious generation, a generation whose heart was not steadfast, whose spirit was not faithful to God." Stubborn, rebellious, and unfaithful. Those three words summarize the outcome that this passage wants you to avoid with your family.

A key principle for grandparents, especially young grandparents: *Wise people learn from their mistakes, but wiser people learn from the mistakes of others.* I hope you learn from the mistakes of grandparents in Psalm 78 and experience the blessing of seeing your family embrace Christ. Failure is a powerful teacher. Here is an opportunity to learn from the failure of others and avoid a similar outcome.

I like the psalmist's tactics. He scanned history, found a pattern of failed family discipleship, and identified key methods that are central to passing on faith to future generations. In essence, he is saying, "If you don't want to raise a stubborn, rebellious, and unfaithful generation, then do these things." Of course, this is not a fail-safe guarantee. We want to avoid determinism that if we do A + B we will get C every time. We recognize that our ultimate hope is not in doing the right things, but in the power of the Gospel. However, we must be obedient to do what God instructs and are wise to utilize biblical methods to pass faith to future generations.

What are three ways grandparents can be intentional to raise future generations who walk with the Lord?

Embrace a multigeneration vision

Psalm 78 provides a four-generation vision for families. As you read Psalm 78:5–6, try to identify the four generations: "He commanded our fathers to teach to their children, that the next generation might know them, the children yet unborn, and arise and tell them to their children." Did you catch the four generations? They are fathers, children, children yet unborn (grandchildren), and their children (great-grandchildren).

God wants us to *think multigenerationally, not mono-generationally*. God isn't just concerned about your children. He wants your grandchildren and great-grandchildren to treasure Christ as well.

For many of us, our vision needs to be expanded. A generation in the Bible is generally believed to be about forty years, which means Psalm 78 gives us a 160-year vision for our family. In a day and age of instant gratification and short-term perspectives, God has given us a large vision to leave a lasting legacy in Christ that outlives us.

How big is your family discipleship vision? Small or large? Temporal or eternal? For a single generation or many? Here are three ways to implement a multigenerational vision with your family:

- Pray that your grandchildren and great-grandchildren will know, love, and serve Jesus. You may never know these individuals by name, but that should not prevent you from praying for them. Prayer is powerful, and God uses it to accomplish His purposes.
- Train your children and grandchildren to disciple their children and grandchildren. When you teach a grandchild a biblical truth, encourage him to teach the same truth to his children and his children's children. Plant the seed in a child's mind that she needs to make disciples of her future family.

- Due to longer life-spans, the opportunity has never been greater for your direct influence on future generations. After I casted a multigenerational vision to a group of grandparents, eighty-seven-year-old Myrtie exclaimed that she was living out Psalm 78, as God gifted her with long life and gave her the opportunity to personally disciple her children, grandchildren, and great-grandchildren.

Do you have a multigenerational vision to impact your family? Or is it limited to an eighteen-year parenting vision that significantly diminishes once a child graduates from high school? Does it extend into grandparenting? Is it outsourced to others such as the church or Christian school? Or is it focused, future-oriented, and multigenerational? The multigenerational vision of Psalm 78 encourages us to live for a time we will not see.

Tell grandchildren the work of God

"Grandpa, tell me a story." You've probably had a similar request from your grandchild. God has hard-wired a hunger for transcendent stories into our lives, and this creates an opportunity for every grandparent to intentionally talk about God. A popular grandparenting journal states, "Grandma. Her stories. Her words." A better perspective is "Grandma. God's story. God's words."

The second component of intentional grandparenting is found in verse 4: "Tell to the coming generation the glorious deeds of the Lord, and his might, and the wonders that he has done." I want you to notice this is a command from God. It highlights an important aspect of your role as a grandparent. God has given you a story to tell your grandchildren about the work of God. According to God, it isn't enough to be a playmate for your grandchild. God expects you to tell future generations about Him.

What does "tell" mean? To tell means to report, to count, to make known, to make a written record. God wants you to report to your grandchildren (the coming generation) what God has done in your life (His glorious deeds). You are an eyewitness with a front-row seat to God's incredible work. God wants you to share your story and talk about your experience with God. God is very specific regarding what you are to talk about with your grandchildren: His deeds, His might, and His wonders.

A prime example is found in Psalm 145:4–12, which provides a glimpse into what grandparents should talk about when they tell their grandchildren about God: "One generation shall commend your works to another, and shall declare your mighty acts. On the glorious splendor of your majesty, and on your wondrous works, I will meditate. They shall speak of the might of your awesome deeds, and I will declare your greatness. They shall pour forth the fame of your abundant goodness and shall sing aloud of your righteousness. . . . They shall speak of the glory of your kingdom and tell of your power, to make known to the children of man your mighty deeds, and the glorious splendor of your kingdom." God wants you to tell your grandchildren the following things about Him:

- Commend His work
- Declare His mighty acts
- Speak of the might of God's awesome deeds
- Declare God's greatness
- Pour forth God's fame
- Sing aloud of God's righteousness

If you have ever wondered what you should talk about with your grandchildren, then let the Bible be your guide. You can be confident because your words are simply a retelling of God's words. I trust that God knows better than anyone what your grandchildren need to hear. Grandchildren need to hear about the character of God, and He made you a messenger. Will you be faithful to deliver that message?

There is an important point to be made here: Grandparents are messengers. Delivering God's message is one of the measures of successful grandparenting. You cannot control how your children or grandchildren respond to God, but you can be obedient and tell the coming generations of the work of God.

Take a moment and evaluate what you talk about with your grandchildren. Do your conversations have a Psalms 78 and 145 orientation to them? Does the work of God saturate your conversation, or is it simply an added seasoning? Is God the King of your talk or a servant to sports, entertainment, fashion, media, or other subjects? Do your grandchildren know, by the way you talk, that Jesus Christ is your greatest treasure, or do they hear a greater love echo forth from your mouth?

The whole of your life should be a daily testimony to the Gospel of Christ and a continuous verification of the eternal truth to your family. God has given you a story to help your family embrace Christ and grow increasingly assured of the things revealed in God's Word. A well-known hymn states, "This is my story, this is my song, praising my Savior all the day long."[1] God has given every grandparent a story. The story is given for His glory, to point future generations to Christ.

Look at life as a big learning experience filled with teachable moments for the purpose of exalting Christ in a way that builds evidence that God exists and that He is who He says He is in the Bible.

Develop your testimony

Telling focuses on describing the work of God and His nature with the hope that your grandchild is captivated by God and worships Him. It is your testimony recounting what God has done and who God is, often in story form. We read, "[He] has established a testimony in Jacob" (Psalm 78:5). God has also established a testimony in you so that you will talk about Him.

How has God worked in your life? How has He proven faithful? How has He provided for you? What have you learned about God throughout your life? Do your grandchildren know about your God-stories? Deuteronomy 6 suggests that you are to talk about this as you go about your day. When you drive, when you rise, when you walk, when you bake cookies, when you watch a movie, when you camp, hike, sew, and fish.

In chapter 9 I will explore testimony as a method used by God to disciple grandchildren, and will also show how personal testimony is used as a tactic of the enemy to destroy the faith of young people.

Teach grandchildren the commands of God

The third aspect of being an intentional grandparent is found in verse 5, "[He] appointed a law in Israel, which he commanded our fathers [grandfathers or forefathers] to teach . . ." If telling looks back, then teaching looks forward. The command to teach suggests that you are trying to shape the grandchild and accomplish specific goals in his or her life.

According to Psalm 78:5, teaching is a central element of a grandparent's role. We read that God "*commanded* our fathers to teach." The Hebrew word for *teach* means to instruct or guide. Guidance is a goal-oriented word. It suggests that there is a specific outcome we are working toward, and teaching is the method to that end. A good guide knows the end destination, leads others on the right path, and instructs along the way.

The enemy wants you to close your mouth because a silent grandparent is a spiritually neutralized grandparent. American society has told a generation of Christian grandparents to remain quiet, and many grandparents have obliged. We quote mantras to justify our silence: "More is caught than taught" and "Preach the Gospel; use words if necessary." Those statements sound good on the surface, but they don't align with Psalm 78. According to God, words are necessary. If the next generation is going to follow the

Lord, we must teach them to do so. Obviously, teaching is more than words, but Psalm 78 makes it clear that at a minimum it includes verbal instruction. We shouldn't hope that Christianity will be caught by osmosis. Christlike example is critical, but it is not exhaustive. Intentional grandparents are teaching grandparents.

Grandparents are to teach God's law, which includes the following:

- God is the source of morality. Your grandchild must develop the firm conviction that God determines right and wrong.
- Grandchildren are born sinful and rebellious. Children are not naturally inclined to submit to authority and must be taught.
- Grandchildren need the Gospel. Every child has broken God's law and needs the free gift of grace through belief in the death and resurrection of Christ.
- Grandchildren need to learn obedience. Your grandchild must be encouraged to live in a manner worthy of the Gospel in accordance with God's commands.

In chapter 11 I will discuss in greater depth how to read the Bible with grandchildren and suggest some key biblical truths that should be taught to a grandchild.

Hope in God

Why commit to telling the works of God and teaching the words of God? Psalm 78:7 provides two reasons:

1. So that future generations will place their hope in God. This is salvation language. God wants your grandchildren to place faith in Him.
2. So that future generations will live in obedience to God. This is sanctification language. God wants your grandchildren to live according to His ways.

An arrow will never hit the mark if it is not aimed. Many grandparents are on a road, but they don't know where it leads. Psalm 78 clarifies the aim and describes the road. It helps you order your time and prioritize your actions.

Teaching and telling are important grandparent roles, but they are not the primary role. They are means to a greater end: a heritage of faith passed from one generation to the next. Society communicates a powerful message that grandparents are extras, not essential to the family. Nothing could be further from the truth. If the history of Israel teaches us anything, it is that grandparents are critical figures in the faith formation of the young.

A picture of intentional grandparenting

If you resonate with Linda, the grandmother from the beginning of the chapter, I want you to be encouraged, because she learned to be an intentional grandparent. Here is what that looks like for her family:

> I try to stay close to them through regular communication. I try to act lovingly and spend time with them. When my children were single, we used to have a big old Sunday pot-roast meal, and I would see them weekly. We had great conversation around food. Now that they are married and in their careers, we do that once a month. Everyone makes a big effort to get here. My husband meets with the guys once a month for breakfast. He goes in with an intentional thought but doesn't make that known. Lately they are reading a book together and discussing it. [The breakfast meal] is not too heavy, but it's enough that we know what is going on and can be aware. If we come across an article, we forward it to them. We also go out to lunch frequently with some of our children and talk about politics, people, and worldview.

I want you to notice three elements of intentionality from Linda's comments. First, Linda *is committed to cultivating a strong relationship with family through regular communication.* How often and in what form do you communicate with your family? In your communication I encourage you to do three things: initiate, be consistent, and adopt flexibility of communication method.

Second, *Linda set a reoccurring time to gather with her family.* One of the problems for many grandparents is that they do not have pre-set, reoccurring dates on the calendar with their family. Every time the family gets together it is a floating, one-time event, and trying to coordinate the calendars of multiple busy families is frustrating and difficult.

Third, *utilize food as a secret weapon.* Notice how much of what Laura does revolves around food? Pot-roast meals, men's breakfasts, and lunch. Use food strategically and to your advantage.

I hope Linda's approach was helpful for you. Her methods are not exhaustive and they are not the same methods all grandparents have to utilize, but sometimes it helps to see how others engage with family.

God designed grandparents to have a vital role in a grandchild's faith development. I want you to take your cues regarding the role of grandparenthood from the Bible and not from culture. A grandparent's main role is not to spoil or be a companion to their grandchild. A grandparent's purpose is not to indulge themselves during the last third of their life. God has given grandparents the role of transferring faith in Christ to future generations. May you give yourself fully to the task of telling the works of God and teaching the words of God so that future generations will put their hope in God and keep His commands.

Grand Chat

1. Read Psalm 78:8 and skim the rest of the chapter for references to rebellion or disobedience. What can we learn from

the mistakes of previous generations as we seek to pass faith on to our family?

2. Read Psalm 78:5–6. How many generations are listed? What are the implications for grandparents? Would you say your family discipleship vision is small or large? Temporal or eternal? For a single generation or many?

3. Read Psalm 78:4. What instruction does God give grandparents in this verse? Share with the group an example of God's work in your life. Have you shared your God-stories with grandchildren? If so, what encouragement or advice can you share with others?

4. Read Psalm 78:5. What are grandparents commanded to do in this verse? Share one or more ways you have verbally taught your grandchildren the truths of the Bible.

5. Read Psalm 78:7. What are the two goals of grandparenting? Why is it important to understand these outcomes?

6. Evaluate your understanding of the role of a grandparent according to the Bible. Do your actions as a grandparent reflect what you see in Psalm 78? Does anything need to change in how you are interacting with family or the priorities in your life?

7. What can we learn from Linda's example of intentionality? Are there any ways you can become more intentional with your family?

8

Three Deficiencies in Christian Families

An Opportunity for Grandparents

Grandparents are needed today more than ever. There is a battle raging for the heart and mind of your family, and it is urgent that you understand your biblical role, recognize the powerful messages of culture, and embrace the Bible's methods to reach and disciple your children and grandchildren so that they treasure Jesus and live for Him.

To help you understand why your role is important, it is critical to recognize three deficiencies in Christian families today: family discipleship, biblical worldview, and church involvement.

Family Discipleship

Every grandparent needs clarity on an important question. *How much discipleship is happening in your child's home?* You need clarity so that you know how best to spiritually invest as a grandparent. Adult children who take their role seriously and are actively discipling their children can be supported, encouraged, and equipped to continue faithfully raising children in the Lord. Children who are not actively discipling present an opportunity for grandparents to encourage adult children to nurture the faith of grandchildren, but also to invest more heavily as a disciple-maker directly with grandchildren.

Unfortunately, the number of Christian parents who disciple their children is low. A Barna study found, "A majority of parents do not spend any time during a typical week discussing religious matters or studying religious materials with their children . . . parents typically have no plan for the spiritual development of their children; do not consider it a priority, have little or no training in how to nurture a child's faith."[1]

I know that's not exciting news, but I point it out because we often assume parents are actively discipling children when the reality is that many parents are doing little on a weekly basis to nurture a child's faith outside of mealtime or bedtime prayers and the occasional faith-based conversation.

I share this as a call to action, not to cause alarm. My hope is to encourage you to informally assess, not assume, and to be active, not passive, in discipleship. I encourage you to ask your adult child two simple questions about parenting: *How is it going?* and *Is there anything I can do to help?*

Deficient family discipleship is one of the critical reasons grandparents are needed. You are in a better position than any pastor or person to encourage an ambivalent adult child to prioritize the discipleship of children.

Biblical Worldview

Grandparents should seek an answer to another important question: *What does your grandchild believe to be true?* This is important to ask because alarmingly high numbers of children raised in Christian homes do not know what the Bible teaches or why they should believe it. Lots of young Christians are unable to explain the Christian faith and don't believe basic truths of Christianity. Woodrow Kroll calls it "an epidemic in New America."[2] When young people encounter a competing belief system, many are unable to defend their faith, doubts about Christianity take root, and unbelief grows.

Grandparents Gary and Cheryl understand the need to train grandchildren with a biblical worldview. They told me, "It is critical that they hear, see, and observe grandparents that have a godly, biblical worldview." Cheryl said, "The idea that I can just be friends with them right now and then when I'm gone that will be fine, is not sufficient."

Gary and Cheryl are correct. Grandparents have the potential to significantly shape the beliefs of grandchildren. Barna studies have found that "a person's worldview is primarily shaped and is firmly in place by the time someone reaches the age of thirteen; it is refined through experience during the teen and early adult years; and then it is passed on to others during their adult life. Such studies underscore the necessity of parents and other influencers being intentional in how they help develop the worldview of children."[3]

How can you help grandchildren develop a biblical worldview?

You can help them understand and defend the essential truths of the Christian faith. Children need apologetics training to establish them in their faith. In a post-Christian society, your grandchild is going to face strong opposition and competing belief systems, and unless the child is rooted in the Bible, she will absorb the ideas of our day and assimilate the beliefs of our culture.

Grandparenting today requires a Colossians 2:6–8 mindset:

> As you received Christ Jesus the Lord, so walk in him, rooted and built up in him and established in the faith, just as you were taught, abounding in thanksgiving. See to it that no one takes you captive by philosophy and empty deceit, according to human tradition, according to the elemental spirits of the world, and not according to Christ.

According to this passage, we're aiming for rooted kids who are built up and established in faith. In addition, we are to train children to defend their faith against deceptive and competing belief systems. Two deceitful philosophies that children are captivated by today are secular humanism (man is god) and socialism (government is god). Another, Islam, becomes more popular every year. Familiarize yourself with them; learn what they teach and why they are deficient, and be able to point out these arguments when you see them in education, media, or culture.

The strategy Paul provides is simple: Teach the core truth of Scripture so that a Christian is established in faith, then introduce a competing belief system and dismantle it by exposing why it is false. When I teach kids, I call this the Bible's big truth and the world's big lie.

So what, exactly, is a biblical worldview? It is a set of beliefs, values, and assumptions based on the Bible that shape how we live. It is another way to describe and define discipleship. Worldview puts the spotlight on two areas the Bible highlights as critical: what we believe and how we live.

A basic framework for a biblical worldview can be summarized in four words: creation, rebellion, salvation, and restoration.

- *Creation*: A sovereign God created the world and everything in it, including people who are made in His image, for His own glory.
- *Rebellion*: Humanity turned away from God, becoming totally depraved and choosing to live for themselves rather than His glory; as a result it came under the curse of sin.
- *Salvation*: God provided a way to save people from sin through the life, death, and resurrection of Jesus.
- *Restoration*: Jesus reigns as King over all and is preeminent over His everlasting kingdom, where we will join Him and where He will make everything new.

These four truths provide the foundation for deep and lasting faith to develop. Each truth has a competing faith-busting philosophy that children must recognize and reject. Children are taught evolution rather than creation; relativism rather than God's law; world religions rather than salvation by faith through Christ; and to value the temporal over the eternal. These four truths answer many of the big questions children ask, such as, "Where did I come from?" "Why am I here?" "Who am I?" "What went wrong with the world?" "What is the solution?" "What is the purpose of life?" "What happens in the future?"

Young people are hungry for truth and are searching for answers. They desire open and honest face-to-face conversations. Young people want real answers and are attracted to authenticity. Due to an overabundance of information, young people do not know what information is trustworthy, so they have a prove-it-to-me mindset. One of the most compelling proofs for young people is an authentic life. The grandparent who speaks truth in love and practices what he or she preaches is incredibly influential in a young person's life.

You must view yourself as an apologist to your family. You have the critical job of persuading your grandchildren to believe the Word of the God and submit to the Son of God. Grandchildren need to embrace the inerrancy, authority, and sufficiency of Scripture as well as the exclusivity, supremacy, and resurrection of Jesus Christ. Grandparents are needed to help children and grandchildren develop a biblical worldview.

Church Involvement

Parents struggle to make disciples of their own children and heavily depend on the church to be the primary discipleship influence in their children's lives. There are three problems with this approach. First, it is not the church's role to raise children and be the primary disciple-maker in their lives. Second, a high percentage of families are not going to church consistently. Third, many churches offer an entertainment-based, Disney-like program for children.

There has been a changing pattern of church attendance by families. Larry Fowler, author of *The Question Nobody Asks About Our Children*, has observed a shift in the frequency of children's church. Larry studied the frequency of attendance for children at evangelical megachurches and discovered that children attend church an average of twenty to twenty-five hours per year. Larry states,

> There are 168 hours in a week and we assume we get one of them. That realization has prompted the popularity of the phrase, "Make Sunday the best hour of the children's week." But 1 in 168 is not much; it is also not reality. In reality, we don't get 1 in 168, we get 1 in 336—or even less. Extrapolated over a longer period of time, we find the average child in our church attends 25 hours a year or less.[4]

Why is this information helpful? First, you should enthusiastically champion the church, encourage your children and grandchildren to prioritize weekly corporate worship with a local congregation as a nonnegotiable, and continually speak of the importance of faithful church involvement in the life of the believer. Infrequent church involvement is not only disobedient to God, but negatively impacts faith development of children, discourages lifelong habits of corporate worship, and prevents young people from developing strong Christian community.

Second, Larry's findings are a reminder that we should not rely on the church to be the primary disciple-maker of children. We need to reject the idea that if children attend church enough they will build strong and lasting faith. The church is given the role of equipping families to raise children in the Lord and supplementing the discipleship efforts of families—not to be the primary place where a child's faith is developed. The attendance model in which we outsource the discipleship of children to pastors is not biblical, and in many cases it's not offering much in the way of spiritual substance either. Jonathan Morrow, director of cultural engagement at Impact 360 Institute, made this observation about how the church ministers to children today:

> We create Disney World-like environments for them in our churches, and then wonder why they have no resilience in faith or life. Students are entertained but not prepared. They've had a lot of fun but are not ready to lead. When the pressure to conform is turned up, Christian teenagers tend to wilt if they do not have the confidence that only comes from knowing why they believe what they believe.[5]

Disney-like environments are common and have proven insufficient to train young people to understand, defend, and live out their faith. Morrow states, "We need to stop pretending that if we entertain teenagers then they will stick around after they graduate. . . . And we need to stop pretending that a few minutes of a moralistic, watered down Bible lesson on a Sunday morning will prepare them to stand firm in their faith. In short, teenagers need a grown-up worldview, not coloring book Jesus."[6]

What does this mean for you as a grandparent? Hopefully this serves as a wake-up call to remind you that your role is needed and necessary. It is a call to motivate you to action. Being a playmate or companion to your grandchildren is not sufficient to encourage a deep, lasting, and Gospel-shaped faith.

I'll summarize the problem I've highlighted in this chapter with two phrases: *disciple-light homes* and *Disney-like churches*. In general, families offer limited discipleship at home, rely on church more, and attend church less. Meanwhile, churches encourage a church-centered discipleship model while offering more fun and less substance. This doesn't even begin to take into account the 16,000 hours children spend in educational settings from kindergarten through twelfth grade where secular humanistic thought prevails, what they absorb from the many hours every day through media, or the influence of their peer group. Is it any wonder that we are losing our children and that lifelong faith remains a challenge?

American culture has changed significantly, and your grandchildren face a serious spiritual battle. Your grandchildren need to be taught truth and be able to ask tough questions; they must work through honest doubts, enter into challenging conversations, and learn to defend their faith.

Satan is real. He hates your children and grandchildren. He is a roaring lion. He wants to deceive, devour, and destroy families. Lions are more likely to attack those who are isolated and vulnerable. The individualistic nature of American culture creates a ripe environment for young people to be isolated from significant adult relationships and to be vulnerable to the deception and attacks of the enemy. Grandparents must prioritize active, intentional engagement with their family.

What does your grandchild believe? If you don't know, you should ask. What can you do to build your grandchild's trust in God's Word? How have you helped to sharpen their focus on Christ? In what ways can you help your grandchild think and live biblically? One of your goals is to build a firm biblical foundation for your grandchildren. There is a battle raging for our grandchildren's minds and hearts, and grandparents need to join the battle for the next generation. Whoever wants the next generation most will get them!

Grand Chat:

1. Discuss how much discipleship is happening in your child's home. How have you encouraged your children to prioritize the discipleship of their family?

2. Read Colossians 2:7–8. How have you helped your grandchildren develop strong beliefs rooted in the Bible so they are not taken captive by cultural ideas?

3. What is biblical worldview and why is it important for your grandchildren to develop?

4. How often do your children and grandchildren attend church? What can you do to encourage frequent involvement at a Bible-teaching church?

9

The Six Most Important Lessons I've Learned as a Grandparent

BY CAVIN HARPER, PRESIDENT OF THE CHRISTIAN GRANDPARENTING NETWORK

The day I became a grandfather felt a lot like my first roller coaster ride—thrilling and terrifying at the same time. When I held my newborn grandson for the first time, I felt an exhilaration I cannot adequately describe.

To be sure, there were other exhilarating moments, such as the day I married the love of my life and the day my first child was born. Yet this was something more. I don't know how to describe it. It was like the difference between your first time flying in a plane and your first parachute jump out of one.

The terrifying side of things was rooted in my wondering what it all meant. What does it mean to be a grandfather? Do I have what it takes, whatever that is? How will I help this child navigate this rapidly changing world? When he's a teenager, will he think me irrelevant—an old man in a rocking chair, unable to relate to his world?

Even more troubling was wondering whether the sobering reality of Judges 2 would be repeated in his time.

> After that whole generation [Joshua and Caleb's generation] had been gathered to their fathers, another generation grew up, who knew neither the Lord nor what He had done. . . . They forsook the Lord, the God of their fathers. . . . They followed and worshiped various gods of the peoples around them.
>
> Judges 2:10–12 NIV1984

Would my grandchildren grow up not knowing the God of the Bible and His Gospel? *Not on my watch*, I prayed. *Lord, please don't let that happen on my watch.*

The troubled feelings started me on a journey to unpack what God says about grandparenting. I could not find a church or family ministry that talked about grandparenting, even though the Bible has much to say about it. The Christian Grandparenting Network was birthed out of a desire to know more.

One of the first things we did was launch GrandCamps, a multi-day faith adventure for grandparents and their grandchildren. It became a hands-on laboratory to learn how to put God's instructions for building a legacy worth outliving us into practice. We spurred one another to be intentional and encouraged each other to not give up, for our God is with us.

It's been anything but a perfect journey. I continue to learn and grow. Out of my successes and failures in this grandparenting journey I have learned a few important lessons. Here are six of the most important; I hope they encourage you in your journey.

Lesson 1: Being a good grandparent is not good enough.
Grandma argued, "But my grandchildren will not love me or want to visit me if I don't let them do things they can't do at home. That's what good grandparents do." Her daughter had asked her to cut back on junk food, endless TV time, and late nights when

the grandchildren visit. As parents, they paid the price when the children came home.

"Mom, if you think your grandchildren love you because you let them do those things, you're sadly mistaken. You can't bribe them to love you."

That daughter was right. If our grandchildren love us only because we give them stuff or let them do things they normally are not allowed to do, something is terribly wrong. Grandchildren don't need grandparents to be best friends or comrades, with Mom and Dad viewed as common enemies. Grandchildren need grandparents they can imitate as they grow into adults.

Yes, they need our love and affection, but they also need to know Christ's love through us. Josh Mulvihill is right when he says, "Your grandchildren need the Good News more than they need good gifts from you." That's a lesson every grandparent needs to learn.

I learned that my prime objective is to show them how much they are loved by faithfully proclaiming the Gospel with my mouth and my life. I want my life to reflect the transforming power of the Gospel by the way I love them as God's image-bearers. I have enjoyed lots of good times with my grandkids. We've built some great memories together, but if my legacy is limited to good times, that legacy matters little.

I can't assume someone else is telling them the Good News. Even if their parents or teachers are doing a good job, my voice is still critical. I need to boldly share my faith journey with them.

Action Step: Be alert for opportunities to share the Gospel with your grandchildren from very early ages. Tell them your faith story and how the Gospel has transformed you. It's never too late to share the Good News.

Lesson 2: My soul's condition shapes the impact of my legacy.
Moses warned the parents and grandparents of his day to take responsibility for telling the next generations of God's faithfulness.

"Only be careful, and watch yourselves closely" (Deuteronomy 4:9 NIV). I like the New American Standard Bible translation best: "Keep your soul diligently."

What does that mean?

Four things are necessary for soul diligence:

1. *A guarded heart.* The writer of Proverbs advises, "Above all else, guard your heart, for it is the wellspring of life" (Proverbs 4:23 NIV1984). My heart is essential because out of it comes what is most important in my life. It reveals what I treasure. Jesus said, "Where your treasure is, there your heart will be also" (Matthew 6:21). My grandchildren will know what I treasure most, and that will be the legacy I leave them.

2. *A guarded mind.* I easily get uptight about some of the things I see my grandchildren viewing on their smartphones and iPads. I'm not always as attentive to what I let into my mind. What do I watch on TV? What do I follow on Facebook that contributes to unhealthy thinking? How much of my thought life focuses on what is true, right, pure, praiseworthy, excellent, and noble? How much is shaped by today's cultural vulgarities? I have learned that guarding my mind demands intentionality about two things. First, I must grow in my knowledge of what is true through daily immersion in the Word of God. Second, I must keep myself from rationalizing what is not appropriate.

3. *A guarded mouth.* Paul states, "Do not let any unwholesome talk come out of your mouths, but only what is helpful for building others up according to their needs, that it may benefit those who listen" (Ephesians 4:29 NIV). I want my grandchildren to hear words from me that speak blessing and life, rather than criticism and negativity. I'm not suggesting we look the other way when wrong thinking surfaces, but that we be careful about the words we speak. The most

important words we may need to say might be, "I was wrong. Will you forgive me?"

4. *A guarded life.* Our words and actions should match. When I tell my grandchildren to treat others with kindness and then I speak poorly about someone I don't agree with, what message does that send? If our life is shaped by the Gospel of Christ, then transparency, integrity, and blessing will impact how we live.

Action Steps:
1. Make Psalm 139:23–24 a daily prayer.
2. Establish a regular time for reading and studying God's Word.
3. Set guidelines for what you watch on TV or how you use social media.
4. Read more of the Bible and other good books worth reading.

Lesson 3: I don't have all the answers.

I have been around the block a few times, but I certainly don't know everything. I don't have all the answers. Neither do you. I'm learning not to get bent out of shape when I don't know the answer to something. If I don't know, I'll do my best to find answers and include my grandchildren if possible. I learn from my grandchildren. I have wisdom and life lessons to pass on, yet I try not to take my opinions too seriously these days. You see, pride really does go before a fall.

Action Steps: When your grandchildren ask you something you don't know, admit it. Ask them to help you to find an answer. When you learn something from your grandchildren, tell them how grateful you are God used them to teach you something new.

Lesson 4: Providing a safe place is more important than proving my point.

It took me a while, but I now realize my grandchildren don't need my wisdom as much as they need my assurance. Grandchildren need the assurance that I'm a safe person with whom they can discuss the hard issues and not be judged, preached at, or shamed.

Ahh . . . but be careful what you read into that. I'm not proposing we avoid speaking what's true. Discipleship is about speaking truth and helping another walk in it. Effective discipleship requires trust, which creates a safe place to express doubts and process questions.

My grandchildren know I care because I listen well. Because I listen, they know they can trust me. Because they trust me, they want to hear what I have to say. I don't need to prove I'm right, although I'm there to help them learn what is right and true. Listening leads to trust, which creates the opportunity to speak into their life.

Action Step: "Be quick to listen, slow to speak and slow to become angry" (James 1:19 NIV). Here are five questions I frequently ask:

1. Will you please explain what you mean by that? (define terms)
2. Where did you get your information about _____?
3. How do you know it's true? What led you to this conclusion?
4. What if you're wrong?
5. What if you're right?

Lesson 5: My life is short, but my legacy is not.

I am confronted daily with the reality of my mortality. The last thirty years passed with a blink of the eye. What remains will be gone in a flash. Life is short. Never miss an opportunity to speak a word of blessing, pray earnestly for your grandchildren, share God's goodness and grace, or tell your grandkids, "This is the day the Lord has made, let's find every reason to rejoice and be glad in it."

I have an earnestness I did not have in my younger years to seize opportunities because I know how quickly the years fly past. I try to speak life-giving words to my grandchildren. I want the legacy I leave to be one filled with words of blessing. I long for my life to scream, "Christ is my all-satisfying treasure!" When the sun sets, I don't want any regrets.

Action Step: Number your days. If you knew you only had a week to live, would you change how you live each day? Why not make those changes now?

Lesson 6: Nothing is more important than praying for my grandchildren.

I remember churches all over the land filling with people crying out to God after the attacks of September 11, 2001. Many of those same churches are empty today when a prayer meeting is scheduled.

Christians often treat prayer as one of their last resorts, turning to it after all other options have been exhausted. Prayer is not my last resort, it is my first resort. It is the first line of offense and defense on behalf of my grandchildren and others.

We are in a battle, not against flesh and blood, but against invisible principalities and powers in the heavenly realms. The spiritual realm is not fiction. It's real. Prayer is our most powerful weapon. We must use it and believe that God is able to do more than we can possibly imagine or think.

God welcomes us coming to Him with daily needs. Even so, I know how prone I am to spend more time praying for the daily bread stuff than about things that matter for eternity, thy kingdom come, thy will be done concerns. Both are important, but kingdom concerns are forever.

Action Steps:
1. Take prayer seriously. Get a free *Scriptures to Pray* download to help you pray daily for your grandchildren at christiangrand parenting.net.

2. Ask other grandparents to join you in a Grandparents@Prayer (G@P) Group. The two-or-more principle of Matthew 18:20 is powerful, so link hands and pray.
3. Tell your grandchildren you are praying for them, but also pray *with* them when you can.

A Final Word

These six lessons do not guarantee a specific outcome, but they do increase the likelihood that our grandchildren will choose to walk in the truth. Even if you already know and practice these things, it's good to be reminded now and then.

"I will make every effort so that after my departure you may be able at any time to recall these things" (2 Peter 1:15). That's what this is—a reminder to forge a legacy that matters for generations to come. One day, perhaps, we will join that great cloud of witnesses looking down at the fruit that has blossomed and reproduced because of the legacy we built on the foundation of the Gospel of Jesus Christ. What a day of rejoicing that will be!

PART 3

DISCIPLESHIP PRACTICES

As we have seen, God clearly defines a grandparent's role. According to the Bible, grandparents are disciple-makers who are given the responsibility of passing on a heritage of faith in Christ to future generations.

The question for us now is *how* should we do that? What methods should you to use to pass on your faith in Christ and grow mature followers of Jesus?

You probably have heard someone say that when it comes to parenting or grandparenting, there are no simple formulas or surefire methods. This statement sounds spiritual, but it is not scriptural. I want you to think seriously about the statement that God provides no surefire methods for grandparenting. If someone is trying to make the point that there are no guarantees, we can agree with that. God is sovereign over salvation, not us. However, if God has not given us discipleship methods to raise grandchildren to maturity in Christ, then where are grandparents to learn how to grandparent? Should we look to "successful" grandparents? The latest research? Ask our children or grandchildren?

God has given us grandparenting methods, and to learn what they are, we must understand the doctrine of sufficiency. What does it mean that the Bible is sufficient? The sufficiency of Scripture means that the Bible provides everything needed for salvation in Jesus, growth into Christlikeness, and obedience to God's commands. The Reformers called this *sola Scriptura*, which translates to "Scripture alone."

The doctrine of sufficiency is found in 2 Timothy 3:15–17 (emphasis added): "the sacred writings . . . are able to make you wise for salvation through faith in Christ Jesus . . . that the man of God may be complete, *equipped for every good work*." Peter makes the same claim when he says that God "has given us *everything* we need for life and godliness" (2 Peter 1:3 NIV1984, emphasis added). The key words in these verses are *every* and *everything*. God has given us everything we need in order to do what He has commanded us in the Bible.

Let's apply the sufficiency of Scripture to grandparenting. Not only does God define *what* a grandparent is to do, but He also describes *how* a grandparent is to make disciples and pass on faith. God doesn't call grandparents to a task without telling them how to accomplish the outcomes He desires.

If the Bible were all that we had, it would be enough to teach us how to grandparent so that grandchildren come to faith in Jesus and grow as disciples of Christ. The sufficiency of Scripture means that we don't need extra-biblical sources to figure out how to grandparent. The sufficiency of Scripture does not mean the Bible is exhaustive. The sufficiency of Scripture doesn't mean we cannot benefit from additional sources outside the Bible, but it does mean that they are secondary and should never be the primary authority or used as a substitute for the Bible.

Does the Bible shape your perspectives and practices on grandparenting? That's the critical question. Or do you look to other sources to determine how to grandparent? Every person looks to an authority on grandparenting; this determines what we do and how we do it.

I have discovered that a high percentage of Christians do not understand how to utilize the Bible for everyday living. Many Christians turn to social media, research, or psychology, or they pragmatically copy the methods of others. The good news is that God provides in the Bible everything we need to know to be a good and godly grandparent.

Our task in this section is to explore eight biblical methods grandparents can utilize to help grandchildren grow spiritually.

If you turned to this section of the book without reading the portion on the biblical role of grandparents, I encourage you to go back and begin there. The methods I share are simply the means to implement your role. If you are unclear about your role, the impact of the methods may be diluted or eventually substituted for non-biblical approaches.

10

Discipleship Practices Every Grandparent Can Do (Part 1)

Four Biblical Methods to Implement

Andrew's hand shot up minutes into a grandparenting seminar and he asked, "How do I help my grandchildren grow spiritually?" After exploring further, I learned that Andrew was inspired by what he was learning about his God-designed role as a grandparent and wanted some practical ways to help his grandchildren develop a deep and lasting faith in Christ. For the answer, we will look to Scripture.

What Is Your Priority?

Colossians 1:28–29 is the passage I turn to when I talk to grandparents about spiritual growth: "Him [Jesus] we proclaim, warning everyone and teaching everyone with all wisdom, that we may present everyone mature in Christ. For this I toil, struggling with all his energy that he powerfully works within me."

Here are a few key points from Colossians 1:28–29:

- *Paul's single-minded focus is Christlike maturity.* While this passage does not speak directly to grandparenting, it speaks to the priorities of all Christians, including grandparents.
- *Paul provides three methods to help individuals mature spiritually*: Gospel-proclamation, warning, and biblical teaching.
- *Spiritual growth requires significant effort.* Paul's exact language of "toil" and "struggling" conveys this. Paul reminds us in verse 29 that it takes work to mature in Christ. The second half of this verse tells us that spiritual growth is not a result of willpower, but God's power working to transform us into the likeness of Jesus.

The key principle for grandparents is this: *Your grandchild's maturity in Christ is your priority.* Paul's ultimate goal is to see everyone presented as mature in Christ. The word *everyone* is repeated three times and includes children and teens, which means this passage is applicable to grandparenting. It isn't enough to see grandchildren grow up to be successful, happy, and responsible adults. Of course that is good, but Paul tells us the ultimate goal is *maturity in Christ*.

The word *maturity* here means ripeness of character. Paul closely connects maturity with Jesus. To be mature is to have Christlike character. Biblical maturity is equivalent to growth into the likeness of Jesus, which means we are only as mature as we are like Jesus in certain areas of our life. You can generally measure your children's and grandchildren's maturity in Christ using the fruits of the Spirit. Each fruit of the Spirit presents an opportunity for you to help your children or grandchildren grow in spiritual maturity. How are you helping your grandchildren become more patient, more holy, more self-controlled, more loving?

Paul states, "For this I toil." All grandparents toil for something. The question is whether or not you are toiling for the right thing. So let me ask you a weighty question: What are you toiling for as a grandparent? What do you hope to accomplish in the lives of your family members? How do you complete the sentence, "I want _____ for my grandchildren"? First and foremost, God calls you to work hard so your children and grandchildren mature in Christ. Toiling for anything other than your family's maturity in Christ is the wrong focus. Can you say with Paul that your aim is to "present [your children and grandchildren] mature in Christ. For this I toil"?

The word *toil* is an agricultural word, which creates the picture of a farmer cultivating a field so that crops can grow and bear fruit. A farmer prepares the field and does everything possible to encourage growth. There are many factors the farmer can't control, such as rainfall, sunshine, and severe weather, which means he must trust God for the results.

Grandparents are like farmers. We plant the seed of the Gospel, water with biblical truths, remove weeds that would hinder growth, and God does the growing (1 Corinthians 3:6). The farmer learns specific skills or methods, such as planting, watering, and weeding to encourage crops to grow. Like a farmer, there are certain methods you can learn that will encourage spiritual growth toward maturity in Christ. That is what we will explore next.

Here are four ways to help your grandchildren grow in maturity in Christ.

Ask Questions

A key biblical method to grow the faith of future generations is question-asking. Your goal is twofold: *Become an askable grandparent, and become skilled at the art of asking good questions.* Use questions to create serious spiritual dialogue, build a strong relationship, and discover what grandchildren believe.

The spiritual practice of question-asking is seen regularly in the Old and New Testaments. God commanded families in the Old Testament to practice traditions, eat specific foods, and erect stone pillars for the purpose of generating curiosity so that young people would ask questions that would encourage spiritual growth (Exodus 12:26-27 and Joshua 4:6-7).

The art of asking good questions is seen regularly in wisdom literature. The psalmist asks a young person, "How can a young man keep his way pure?" then answers with a biblical truth, "By living according to [God's] Word" (Psalm 119:9 NIV). The book of Ecclesiastes contains more than twenty-five questions to encourage deep thought about the purpose of life. For example, the author of Ecclesiastes asks, "For apart from [God] who can eat or who can have enjoyment?" (Ecclesiastes 2:25).

The author in Proverbs asks life application questions to help young people make wise choices (1:22; 8:1), avoid laziness (6:6–11), pursue sexual purity (6:28), seek holiness (20:9), discern future plans (20:24), and understand suffering (23:29). The author of Proverbs explains one reason for asking questions: "Have I not written for you thirty sayings of counsel and knowledge, to make you know what is right and true, that you may give a true answer to those who sent you?" (Proverbs 22:20–21).

Jesus mastered the art of asking good questions and used them regularly. In the four Gospels, Jesus asked over one hundred questions. That is significant and reveals how important this method was. Jesus asked hard, probing questions, forcing people to think deeply; revealed motives; and taught truth. Jesus used questions like an oyster uses a grain of sand. The unexpected question lowered defenses and worked as a catalyst to produce a pearl. Jesus also used questions to cause individuals to reflect and respond. Some of Jesus' questions were open-ended, such as "Who do you say that I am?" (Mark 8:29). Other questions were yes or no questions to determine what a person believed: "Do you believe that I am able to do this?" (Matthew 9:28).

Like the author of Proverbs, ask questions with intentionality to help your grandchildren know what is right and true.

Like the author of Ecclesiastes, ask questions to encourage your grandchildren to ponder the big questions of life.

Like the families in the Old Testament, strategically place things around your home to generate God-centered discussion.

Like Jesus, ask questions that reveal the heart and encourage grandchildren to think deeply about the identity of Christ.

Key tools

Use a catechism. A catechism is a systematic approach to teaching biblical truth using questions and answers. Catechisms are a common historical method to train the next generation. I highly recommend you keep a catechism at home for use with grandchildren.

There are many good catechisms available. For preschool and grade-school children I recommend *My 1st Book of Questions and Answers* by Carine MacKenzie. The book is arranged around important themes, such as God, man, sin, salvation, and the Ten Commandments. It is simple enough for a two-year-old to understand but meaty enough for grade-school students to enjoy. Children are asked simple questions, such as "Who made you?" The answer is "God," with a reference to Genesis 1:27. We often ask our children three to five questions during dinner and have open-ended discussion about the answer.

The *New City Catechism* is available as a free downloadable app or as a book. It contains one hundred questions, with theologically sound answers, prayers, and video explanations. Timothy Keller was instrumental in creating this catechism, and I've used it successfully with older grade-school students and younger teens. If you have long-distance grandchildren, this catechism could be downloaded by the grandchild and you, with discussion occurring over the phone.

Gather good questions. Good questions can be found everywhere. Be on the lookout for them and add them to your toolkit when you find one. I'll get you started with twenty-five questions:

1. What made you sad or happy today?
2. What was your favorite part of the day?
3. What made you laugh this week?
4. What are you looking forward to this week?
5. What rule was the hardest to follow this week?
6. What is your favorite color, hobby, city, smell, food, vacation, drink, game, sport, movie, show, music group?
7. If you had a safe, what would you keep in it?
8. If you could afford anything at this moment, what would you buy?
9. What is one thing you love about your mother or father?
10. What is the best adventure you've had with a friend?
11. What are three characteristics you look for in a friend?
12. What is an animal that best describes you?
13. What is a lesson you've learned the hard way?
14. What is a memory that makes you laugh?
15. What is something you are afraid of?
16. What is a challenge you are facing?
17. What is a dream you have for the future?
18. If you could change anything in the world, what would it be?
19. If you could go anywhere in the world, where would you go?
20. If you could be anything you wanted, what would you be?
21. If you could ask God any question, what would you ask?
22. If you were stranded on an island, which three people would you want with you?
23. What are you thinking about lately?

24. What has influenced your thinking on this topic?

25. How do you know that is true? What if you are wrong?

Questions are powerful tools that build relationships and challenge thinking. Good questions increase intimacy and cause disequilibrium for deeply held assumptions. A good question reveals the heart, motivates people to learn more, and reminds us of biblical truth. Good questions can unlock the door to your grandchild's heart. Learn to use questions to increase your grandparenting effectiveness.

Blessing

A spoken blessing is an opportunity for a grandparent to share his or her deep affection and desired future for a grandchild. John Trent and Gary Smalley describe *blessing* in the following way: "A family blessing begins with meaningful touching. It continues with a spoken message of high value, a message that pictures a special future for the individual being blessed, and one that is based on an active commitment to see the blessing come to pass."[1]

According to Trent and Smalley, a spoken blessing contains at least three elements: meaningful touch, a message of high value, and a picture of a special future.[2] Let's look at each more closely.

Meaningful touch. Meaningful touch was an important element of blessings in Scripture. Trent and Smalley state, "Each time the blessing was given in the Scriptures, meaningful touching provided a caring background to the words that would be spoken. Kissing, hugging, or the laying on of hands were all part of bestowing the blessing."[3] If you are not someone who normally hugs a grandchild, then a blessing provides you with that opportunity.

Message of high value. Many grandchildren are not verbally encouraged or affirmed often and are in danger of developing low self-worth and pursuing affection from wrong sources. Some grandparents assume family members know they are loved despite rarely communicating affection. Other grandparents believe that being physically present is the blessing. Both are misconceptions. I don't know of a single person who tires of hearing they are loved and valued. Silence is a powerful form of communication. Trent and Smalley state, "The major thing silence communicates is confusion. Children who are left to fill in the blanks when it comes to what their parents think about them will often fail the test when it comes to feeling valuable and secure. Spoken words at least give the hearer an indication that he or she is worthy of some attention."[4] God blessed us by giving us His Son, the Word that "became flesh and dwelt among us" (John 1:14). God is a God of the spoken word, and you should be a grandparent who imitates God's method with your family.

Picture of a special future. The last element of a blessing in the Bible focuses on a child's future. You will bless your grandchild when you recognize his strength or her gifting and speak into ways that God can use his or her special wiring for His good and glory in the future. Trent and Smalley write that we cannot predict the future but, "We can, however, encourage and help them to set meaningful goals. We can also convey to them that the gifts and character traits they have right now are attributes that God can bless and use in the future."[5] Your words need to be accompanied by a commitment to help a grandchild mature in Christ.

Why should you consider blessing your family with a spoken blessing? Here are five reasons:

1. *Modeled by God.* God placed a high value on the spoken blessing by incorporating it into the creation of humanity as well as the baptism and transfiguration of Jesus. What was the first thing God did after creating Adam and Eve? "God *blessed* them. And God said to them, 'Be fruitful and multiply and fill the earth and subdue it'" (Genesis 1:28, emphasis added). Abraham, Isaac, and Jacob blessed their children and grandchildren (Genesis 17:15–17; 27; 49). God

set an example for us when He blessed Jesus at His baptism and transfiguration: "This is my beloved Son, with whom I am well pleased" (Matthew 3:17; 17:5).

2. *A common practice in the Old Testament.* The most famous blessing is the priestly blessing from Aaron to the people of Israel: "The Lord bless you and keep you; the Lord make his face to shine upon you and be gracious to you; the Lord lift up his countenance upon you and give you peace" (Numbers 6:24–26).

3. *A repeated pattern of Scripture.* It was a big event in biblical times to be blessed by your father. Many young people resonate with Esau's heartfelt request, "Bless me, even me also, O my father" (Genesis 27:38). Esau longed to be loved by his father, and Isaac missed an opportunity to encourage his son and build a strong family. A blessing has no mystical or magical power, but it can build intimacy, reduce insecurity, and provide a hope-filled vision for the future.

4. *God's plan for humanity.* God tells Abraham that He will bless the world through his descendants, which ultimately points to Jesus. Genesis 12:3 states, "In you all the families of the earth shall be blessed." To understand this statement we must recognize that all creation and every human lives under the curse of sin. Sin affects everything that exists. Genesis 12:3 reveals God's unfolding plan of salvation through Jesus Christ, the blessing of Abraham, who will reverse the curse through His death and resurrection and finally through His second coming. Those in Christ rejoice that Jesus became the curse for us so we might become the righteousness of Christ, and we live in anticipation that the curse will be reversed so there is no more death, tears, or pain. Our families are full of people who live under the curse, and God has made us agents of blessing by preaching the Gospel and feeding the family flock.

5. *A command to bless the Lord.* God instructs believers to bless the Lord: "Lift up your hands to the holy place and bless the Lord!" (Psalm 134:2). "Bless the Lord, O my soul, and all that is within me, bless his holy name!" (Psalm 103:1).

A blessing is valuable because it creates a time and way to communicate affection and affirmation. If you want to become more intentional in this area, consider utilizing a blessing, as it may provide a vehicle for you to communicate the affection you feel but don't always say. An added value of blessings is that they are powerful due to the forethought required and the formal nature of a spoken blessing. If blessings help you, I encourage you to use them while recognizing that there is no mystical power or required action associated to them in the Bible.

If you would like to speak a blessing to your grandchild, also write it out and give it to your grandchild when finished. They will cherish this gift and return to it throughout life. You might consider including a meaningful passage of Scripture that reflects who your grandchild is or a desired future for the grandchild. Make the time of blessing special and not rushed. May the Lord bless your efforts to impact your children and grandchildren for Christ!

Examples of blessings

Example #1: From Jane Mulvihill to Josh Mulvihill

May you know that God delights in you and loves you.

May you know what a treasure you are to me, to God, and to His kingdom.

May Jesus satisfy your every need and your every desire.

May you always walk in the Spirit.

May you love the Lord your God with all your heart.

May you love the lost into the kingdom.

May you be filled up to overflowing with God's abundant blessings.

Example #2: Given at the birth of a grandchild

Thomas, son of Bruce and Alice, welcome to the Nelson and Harden families. I cannot begin to tell you how much your grandmother and I are thrilled to have you with us. We have anticipated your arrival with great eagerness, and you have not disappointed us at all. Though you came into this world through much hardship and pain, you have been received with much joy and delight! With the same measure of struggle and determination with which you have entered this life, so shall your measure of courage, strength, and perseverance be in the service of your Creator, Lord, and Savior.

You are Thomas, "seeker of truth," and so shall you be a man who passionately seeks after God and His truth with a bold faith. As a man of faith and seeker of truth, you will know the reward and cost of following Christ in a hostile world. With God as your help, may you be strong and courageous, not fearing man, but trusting God with your whole heart.

You are blessed with parents who love you and who love the Lord. They have chosen to build their marriage and family upon the foundation of faith in Jesus Christ as Lord and Savior, a foundation that will not crumble. Learn from their example, heed their instruction, and imitate their faith, for inasmuch as their love grows and endures for one another and the Lord, so shall this blessing be fulfilled in you.

We love you, Thomas, and we promise to pray for you, your parents, and your growth in wisdom, grace, and truth.

With all our love,
Your Proud and Grateful Grandparents

Example #3: Spoken to a grade-school-aged grandchild

Daniel, you are loved, you are special, and God has given you important gifts uniquely planned for His purposes for you. You are an unfinished work in the Master Workman's hands. May you continue to grow in the process He is using to complete the masterpiece He is working in you.

Your Bible namesake (Daniel) was a great man of faith and prayer. He believed God and was willing to trust God faithfully even if it meant he must die. You have a great strength of character, Daniel, and a loyal heart. May you always be loyal to your God and use that heart to serve others well.

We love you, take great delight in you, and will always pray for you. May you always seek and serve the Lord in all you do. And may your heart always be full of God's love, peace, joy and happiness. These things come from God, not the things of the world. Find them and you will find great reward.

With all our love,
Papa and Nana
Matthew 5:16

Intentional Meals

A third method to pass faith on to future generations is the use of intentional meals. God commands parents and grandparents to commit wholeheartedly to teaching the truths of God's Word to future generations and "talk of them when you sit in your house" (Deuteronomy 6:7). What better place to practice "when you sit in your house" than around the table?

A quick glance through Scripture reveals the value of food in the homes of God's people. Food was a means of showing hospitability, a sign that peace existed between those who shared a meal, and was a way to celebrate major family milestones such as Isaac's weaning (Genesis 21:8) or Jacob's wedding (Genesis 29:22). Old Testament families were commanded to utilize food with children to generate spiritual questions as well as teach important truths about God and salvation history (Exodus 12:26). In the New Testament, food becomes symbolic of the death and resurrection of Christ and an object lesson to teach about Christ's work on the cross (Matthew 26:26–28). Jesus gives thanks to God the Father for His provision of bread and models a dependent spirit that families are to imitate when they eat a meal (Mark 14:22).

What makes mealtimes valuable?

An opportunity to connect. Today's families are scattered, busy with activities, often running from place to place. Mealtimes present an opportunity to bring the family together. If your family lives close geographically, be intentional about lunch outings with grandchildren, coffee with children, Sunday dinner at Grandma's, big feasts at holidays, and planned family meals where memories can be made, relationships strengthened, and faith passed on. Here are a couple of tips to make your mealtime successful:

View mealtime as talk time. Eliminate distractions by silencing media devices. Aim for meaningful discussion in which everyone can participate.

Know that food is your secret weapon. Get to know your grandchildren and children's favorite snacks, drinks, and meals, and keep them on hand. Home-cooked meals, grandma's cookies, and special treats are worth the time and money. Good food provides one more reason for your family to come over.

Serve child-friendly food. If you have younger grandchildren, the key to a good family gathering is well-fed and well-rested young ones. Provide healthy sides, snacks, and options that children like. Eat early and eat often. Generally, young children don't do well with late meals.

Accommodate food preferences. If your adult children have different eating habits or preferences than you, accommodate as possible. This may include special diets or food sensitivity needs. Don't make mealtime a battleground; make it the playground that everyone looks forward to and is full of much laughter.

An opportunity to celebrate. There is great value in God-centered family celebrations that draw us together to acknowledge the goodness of God and rejoice in the accomplishment of

His people. God models affirmation when He states, "Well done" for doing good and being faithful (Matthew 25:23). Sam Crabtree, in his book *Practicing Affirmation*, notes,

> Ultimately, all praise belongs to God. But penultimately, praise can and should go to people on the way to ultimately bringing glory to God, who gave those people the grace, gifts, and character they demonstrate.[6]

Let us guard against celebration that elevates a person above God or affirmation without the joyful recognition that God supplied the giftedness that made the accomplishment possible. With God at the center, celebrations become a rich opportunity to praise God and rejoice in the One from whom all blessings flow. Use meals to celebrate God's blessings in the form of life achievements, major milestones, and special holidays as well as new faith in Christ and progression in holiness.

An opportunity to teach. For many grandparents, meals represent a missed opportunity to discuss matters of faith or teach God's Word to grandchildren. Grandparents have often commented that mealtime is chaotic and feels more like a chore to get through rather than a joy to embrace. If you do not intentionally utilize mealtimes as an opportunity to shape beliefs, offer spiritual input, and provide biblical wisdom, then consider these tools to assist you.

Key tools

Our family uses a *You Are Special Today* plate for birthdays, big days, or noteworthy accomplishments. When we celebrate a birthday, we pause for a short time to affirm Christlike virtues and character traits. The red plate is always a welcome addition and the recipient is often grinning from ear to ear.

Invest in a quality table. If you want to spend time around your table, purchase one that is large enough for your family and comfortable enough to encourage people to linger. Paul wrote, "Whether you eat or drink, or whatever you do, do all to the glory of God" (1 Corinthians 10:31). May God be glorified around your table. May your conversations be sweet and your family grow closer to one another and more like Christ.

Prayer

Phyllis approached me with tears in her eyes and a quiver in her voice to ask for help with an issue related to one of her grandchildren. "My teenage grandson is gravitating toward the wrong friends and making poor choices." After a short pause, Phyllis asked, "What can I do?"

I am regularly approached by grandparents who ask what can be done about a challenging family situation. The tendency is to look for a quick solution. The temptation is to feel helpless and throw up our hands in frustration.

God has given grandparents a solution, and it's found in Philippians 4:6: "Do not be anxious about anything, but in everything by prayer and supplication with thanksgiving let your requests be made known to God." Prayer is the greatest answer. It is the first line of defense. Prayer is a wonderful gift to grandparents and for your family.

Prayer is not an extra; it is an essential method to reach and disciple your family. The Bible tells us that Job prayed for his sons every morning and that "this was Job's regular custom" (Job 1:5 NIV). Paul tells Timothy that his faith was passed down from his grandmother Lois and imparted through prayer (2 Timothy 1:5–6). Jesus prioritized prayer by rising early in the morning and prayed for protection over his disciples (Mark 1:35; John 17:15). There is a pattern and a priority to prayer that is noteworthy in the narrative of Scripture.

Sylvia Gunter, author of *For the Family*, states, "Praying for your family is the most vital, unrelenting, frustrating, neglected, and rewarding assignment of a parent."[7] Prayer is vital because the spiritual destiny of your family may depend on it. It is unrelenting as it is a daily habit to be cultivated because the enemy is on a mission to destroy our families. Prayer can be frustrating because after we have prayed long and hard, the rebel has not surrendered or the spiritually dead has not come to life. It is neglected due to busyness or the belief that there is a better solution. Prayer is rewarding when God answers a request.[8]

Praying daily for children and grandchildren is important and should be a priority. If you've ever thought, *All I can do is pray*, then hopefully this is a reminder that prayer is the greater work. It is the means God uses to bring about spiritual transformation. Prayer yields great fruit and is never futile. Prayer should be our first response, never our last resort. Praying grandparents are influential grandparents because they appeal to the One who is all-powerful.

Key tools

If you are looking for prayer help or want to develop a more consistent prayer habit, there are some wonderful prayer tools available to assist you. Here are a few of my favorites:

Praying the Bible is an excellent book that can transform your devotional life. An excellent resource for individuals who find themselves struggling to pray, bored by prayer, or praying repetitive prayers. Donald Whitney teaches readers how to have a meaningful and satisfying prayer life by praying through a passage of the Bible. *Praying the Bible* uses a time-tested method that shows readers how to pray through the Bible one line at a time.

Grandparenting with a Purpose is one of my go-to prayer resources for grandparents. Lillian Penner is the national prayer coordinator for the Christian Grandparenting Network and has written a concise book that provides Scriptures to pray, topics to pray about, and prayer methods. If you are interested in a prayer group for grandparents, consider starting a Grandparents @ Prayer group (G@P group) at your church. Information is available at the Christian Grandparenting Network.

Grandma's Cookie Jar, a website hosted by my friend Lynda Freeman, has some Bible-based prayer resources you may find helpful.

Praying the Bible for Your Kids weaves together with prayer a reading from the Bible, beginning in Genesis and ending in Revelation. The guided prayers are based on the big ideas and basic principles from the highlighted passages.

Grand Chat

1. Read Colossians 1:28–29. What are you toiling for as a grandparent? How do you complete the following sentence? "I want _____ for my grandchildren."

2. Would you consider yourself good at asking questions of your children or grandchildren? Why or why not?

3. Have you given a blessing to your children or grandchildren? How would you like to incorporate a blessing for your grandchildren?

4. How do you use meals as a tool for connecting in a deeper way with your grandchildren? What practical things can you do to make mealtimes a more valuable experience than they currently are?

5. What does praying for your family look like in your life? What steps can you take to begin the process of praying regularly and consistently for your grandchildren?

11

Discipleship Practices Every Grandparent Can Do (Part 2)

Four More Biblical Methods to Implement

In the last chapter we looked at four ways grandparents can help a grandchild mature in faith. Asking questions, intentional meals, blessings, and prayer are methods commonly found in the narrative of Scripture to help future generations embrace Christ. This chapter will explore four additional practices that every grandparent can utilize to disciple grandchildren: communicate wisdom, read and discuss the Bible, tell God-stories, and share the Gospel.

Communicate Wisdom

A reoccurring theme from the book of Proverbs is that young people are prone to making poor choices and need the guidance of older, more mature believers (Proverbs 7:7). Proverbs teaches that young people need wisdom for everyday decisions, such as choosing godly friends, sexual purity, honoring God with money, and a strong work ethic. The wise man in Proverbs 4:5 says to the young person, "Get wisdom, get insight." What does this mean? Why is it important?

What is wisdom?

Wisdom is obedience in action. Jesus stated, "Everyone then who hears these words of mine and does them will be like a *wise man* who built his house upon the rock" (Matthew 7:24, emphasis added). A wise person hears what God says and lives it out. At its most basic level, obedience is a sign of wisdom. For example, God instructs Christians to marry Christians, not unbelievers (2 Corinthians 6:14). A wise Christian seeks a future mate with God's unbending criteria for a spouse in mind. A foolish person knows what God commands but disobeys and does what he or she wants, thinking it will lead to happiness.

Wisdom also means applying God's truth to life. It is moral skillfulness. A wise person has learned how to take a principle of Scripture and apply it to a life situation. Biblical wisdom includes discerning how faith in Christ should work itself out in situations not specifically dealt with in the Bible.

Wisdom begins with the conviction that God's Word provides the practical knowledge for decision-making and direction in life. Paul calls this "spiritual wisdom" and prays that the Colossians would be filled with it in order to know God's will for life (Colossians 1:9). We can know God's will when we have saturated our mind with God's Word. When we have saturated our mind with God's Word, we are able to make wise choices as we live in God's world.

Why is wisdom important for your grandchild?

The book of Proverbs provides three compelling reasons.

1. *Wisdom leads to true and lasting happiness.* Every grandchild is on a quest for happiness, and the Bible tells us where it is found. Proverbs 3:13 states, "Blessed is the man who finds

wisdom." God has hard-wired into all people a desire to be happy, and His prescription for happiness includes wisdom. If you have an unhappy or depressed grandchild it could be that he or she is seeking happiness from the wrong source. If your grandchild does not seek happiness in God, he or she will seek it from a substitute. It will leave them unsatisfied, knowing there must be something more to life.

2. *Wisdom is the path to eternal life and favor with God.* In Proverbs 8:35, wisdom is speaking and says, "Whoever finds me finds *life* and obtains *favor* from the Lord" (emphasis added). If a grandchild does not make it a goal to get wisdom, he or she will suffer grief and death. A lack of wisdom is the headwater of foolish decisions, which result in costly consequences.

3. *Wisdom is extremely valuable.* The grandparent who shares wisdom with a grandchild gives him or her something of immeasurable worth. Proverbs reminds us that wisdom is better than gold and more desirable than silver (Proverbs 16:16). You have a treasure that is better than any financial inheritance, and that is wisdom.

God has placed grandparents in the life of grandchildren to help them make wise decisions. In order to do that, grandparents must know God's Word and know their grandchildren. Grandparents must know God's Word because we are not wise and have nothing to offer apart from Scripture (1 Corinthians 3:18–23). Wisdom is found in the Word of God. The psalmist says that the law of God makes the simple wise (Psalm 19:7). We must apply ourselves to the study of God's Word so that we can disciple grandchildren in decision-making.

Grandparents must know a grandchild intimately in order to speak into a grandchild's decisions and direction in life. Do you know your grandchild? Do you spend regular time with your grandchildren? Does your grandchild trust you and seek your guidance?

Do you know God's Word so that you can apply it to life situations? When direction is needed, you can take a lifetime of experience in God's Word and apply it to a grandchild's life situation.

Key tools

Every grandparent wants to see grandchildren make good choices, grow in wisdom, and live in a God-honoring way. *Wise Up: Ten-Minute Family Devotions in Proverbs* by Marty Machowski is a resource you can use to teach grade-school-aged grandchildren the truths of Proverbs in a quick and enjoyable way. One of the things I appreciate about *Wise Up* is that it is not moralistic, but grounds God's wisdom in the Gospel.

Read and Discuss the Bible

God instructs grandparents to teach grandchildren the truths of Scripture: "Make them known to your children and children's children" (Deuteronomy 4:9). In Psalm 78:5 God commands grandparents to teach multiple generations to obey God's commands.

Throughout church history the primary method to teach and disciple young people has been called family worship. Family worship is the means of introducing children to the truths of Scripture and preparing children for the Christian life. The practice consists of reading the Bible as a family, praying, and praising God through music. If you have not developed the habit of regularly reading and discussing the Bible with your grandchildren, then this is a high-impact priority for you to implement.

Consider a few practical thoughts:

- *Read the Bible, not someone's thoughts about the Bible.* The best devotionals make the Bible the primary source and keep the Gospel central to each section of Scripture. Marty Machowski has written *Long Story Short* and *Old Story New*,

Bible reading plans with discussion questions and prayer. My book *Preparing Children for Marriage* contains fifteen Bible studies you can use with grandchildren on marriage, dating, purity, and sex.

- *Read the entire Bible to children.* The pattern of Scripture is to teach children the deep truths of Scripture. For example, children were not excused when theologically weighty topics were covered in the Colossian or Ephesian church. Children were present to be told to obey parents, and therefore were taught everything contained in these two books.

- *Read briefly.* Remember, they are children. The younger a grandchild is, the shorter their attention span. Don't expect your grandchild to study the Bible like an adult. Try to keep your family reading concise and to the point, but meaningful. Ten minutes is a good amount of time to begin with.

Your goal is to explain the Bible passage clearly and biblically, engage grandchildren in the process, and help them apply God's truth to life.

Teach grandchildren the core truths of Christianity

Grandparents should teach grandchildren of all ages the core truths of the Christian faith with a zeal and consistency that follow the pattern of the Bible. We read of Timothy: "*From childhood* you have been acquainted with the sacred writings, which are able to make you wise for salvation through faith in Jesus Christ" (2 Timothy 3:15, emphasis added). And in Psalms, "*Since my youth*, God, you have taught me, and to this day I declare your marvelous deeds" (Psalm 71:17 NIV, emphasis added).

The pattern of Scripture is for children of all ages to be taught the core truths of the Bible so that they will be firmly rooted in Christ and established in their faith (Colossians 2:7). The following topics should be taught to children of all ages:

The big picture of the Bible

The Bible is not a random collection of people or events. It is a unified whole with one main storyline pointing to, revolving around, and fulfilled in Jesus. There are four major parts of the Bible: creation (Genesis 1–2), rebellion (Genesis 3), salvation (Genesis 4–Revelation 20), and restoration (Revelation 21–22). As you read through the Old Testament, help grandchildren see how it points to Jesus and His covenant of salvation. Jesus himself did this: "Then beginning with Moses and with all the prophets, He explained to them the things concerning Himself in all the Scriptures" (Luke 24:27 NASB).

The primary aim of the Bible is to glorify God, and this happens in salvation and judgment found on every page of the Bible. Read and reread the stories of the Bible to your grandchildren with this in mind. Familiarize them with the main stories, people, and events of the Bible, but not in a way that detaches them from the overall storyline of Scripture. We should call our grandchildren to obey Jesus Christ, and we can use the heroes of the faith as models to imitate, but let our teaching not dissolve into moralistic instruction separated from the Gospel of Jesus or the glory of God.

Teaching the big picture of the Bible accomplishes two things. First, it answers the big questions of life that every young person will ask, such as, Where did I come from? What is the purpose of life? Who am I? What went wrong in the world? Why is there pain and suffering? What is the answer to all the problems? What happens after I die?

Second, it trains young people with a biblical view of life so they have the ability to detect and reject the world's big lies. When you teach creation, it will help to refute evolution and atheism; rebellion contradicts relativism (God determines right and wrong); salvation in Christ counters all other world religions; and restoration addresses the problem of evil (we have hope).

Core truths of the Christian faith

The Bible's word for core truths is *doctrine*. *Doctrine* is simply a word to describe what the Bible teaches. Paul challenges young Timothy to "watch your life and doctrine closely" (1 Timothy 4:16 NIV). Every grandchild needs to understand the core truths of the Christian faith to grow into a man or woman with convictions to follow God.

The two most critical doctrines for grandchildren to learn center on the Word of God and the Son of God. It is a mark of successful grandparenting to teach grandchildren the inerrancy, authority, and sufficiency of the Bible. It should be a high priority for all grandparents to train grandchildren to embrace the supremacy, exclusivity, deity, and lordship of Jesus Christ.

In addition, we must repeatedly (with greater depth as grandchildren age) teach topics such as the character and existence of God; God's design for marriage between one man and one woman; biblical manhood and womanhood; Christ-honoring sexuality; stewardship of time, talents, and treasures; and wise choices based on godly character.

The example of Lois

One grandparent worthy of closer examination is Lois. Lois was the grandmother to Timothy and played an important role in his spiritual life (2 Timothy 1:5). The apostle Paul suggests that Lois taught Timothy the Scriptures from an early age, which became foundational in his following Christ (2 Timothy 3:14–15). Lois is a godly grandparent worthy of imitation. Grandparents might consider three principles for teaching grandchildren:

1. *Early instruction* (2 Timothy 1:5; 3:15). Research reveals that upwards of 80 percent of individuals become Christians before age twelve. The early years are important because children are most moldable at this stage of life.

2. *Frequent instruction* (2 Timothy 3:14). Paul tells Timothy to continue in his firm belief in Christ. Firm belief results from a lot of little conversations over a long period of time that are reinforced at different ages and stages of life.
3. *Biblical instruction* (2 Timothy 3:15). Notice that Timothy is taught the Bible from a young age. There is no substitute for Scripture-based teaching as it is the means God uses for salvation of the young.

Key tools

Donald Whitney has written a concise and practical book called *Family Worship*. I like this book because it can be read in under an hour and provides a quick overview of family worship in the Bible and in church history, and it covers the three primary components of family worship. If you would like to develop the habit of regular, consistent family devotions, this is the book to get.

The Bible's Big Story and *The Whole Story of the Bible in 16 Verses* will help you teach your grandchildren the big picture of the Bible centered on Jesus Christ. *The Bible's Big Story* can be read in one sitting with grade-school children and touches on the main people and themes of the Bible. *The Whole Story of the Bible* is perfect for teens and would make a great gift or could be read and discussed over time.

There are many good resources to teach children and youth the core truths of the Christian faith. For children, I recommend *The Gospel for Children* and *What Does the Bible Say About That?* For teens, I recommend *Bitesize Theology* and *Essential Truths of the Christian Faith*. These books will help you teach the basics of faith in an age-appropriate way.

Tell God-Stories

In Psalm 78 God instructs older generations to tell younger generations the work of God and His nature so that young people set their hope in God and keep His commands. One way of telling God-stories is to create a written record to pass on to your grandchildren. The Bible utilizes this method to encourage future generations to praise God: "Let this be recorded for a generation to come, so that a people yet to be created may praise the Lord" (Psalm 102:18). God has chosen the written Word as the key method to draw us to Christ and deepen our faith (2 Timothy 3:15; Colossians 1:28). Let God's methods be your methods.

A personal testimony

My mother died in 2008 from ALS, so she never had the opportunity in person to influence her grandchildren for Christ. Despite her death, one of the ways my mother's spiritual legacy lives on is through a written testimony. When my mom was very sick, I took two weeks to sit at her feet, ask her questions about her faith in Christ, and record her answers. Here is a sample of the questions I asked:

- Tell me about your quiet time. What does it consist of?
- Tell me about how you pray. What do you pray for?
- What are some of the most meaningful passages of Scripture to you?
- What is your favorite verse? Book of the Bible? Hymn?
- What book of the Bible do you find yourself reading the most?
- What are some of your favorite family memories?
- Tell me what you learned in all your years of marriage and parenting. What should I know?
- Tell me what you learned in a lifetime of service to God.
- What do you want your grandchildren to know about you?
- What was important to you in life? What did you value?
- Tell me about how you became a Christian.

- Tell me how God worked in your life.
- What life wisdom can you share related to money, relationships, good decisions, bad decisions?

When I asked my mom what she wanted her grandchildren to know about her, she said, "I want them to know that I was a person who walked with her God and had an ongoing intimate relationship with Him. I want them to know that I lived in light of eternity; that I was a great mom to her kids. They should know that I like to cook and bake, even clean, dance, and read." From time to time we read my mother's testimony, and it is an encouragement to pursue Christ. I hope my mother's example gives you a vision, if only a small one, to tell your grandchildren about the work of God in your life.

I have two cautions when it comes to telling stories.

First, guard against being a glory thief. Glory thieves make themselves the center of attention, rather than God. They are skilled at the art of turning conversations to focus on themselves. God is a jealous God and does not share His glory. Thus, it is a serious matter to exalt oneself at the expense of God in the eyes of others. Make God the focal point, not your accomplishments or failures. You are not the point; you are the pointer. God's goodness is overflowing in your life, and every good gift is an opportunity to point to the Gift Giver and make much of God.

Second, test what is meant when others talk about being a family historian or storyteller. In grandparenting literature, grandparents are often given these roles. As with any half-truth, it sounds good because it is partially correct. The question is, whose story are you telling? Yours or God's? Your stories have a purpose. Your family history exists to be a vessel to declare the mighty acts of God, His wondrous works, and His greatness as displayed in your life. God is real; the Bible is true, Jesus is the risen Savior, and you can testify to this reality.

Story as an apologetic

Personal story is being used to persuade your grandchildren to abandon their Christian beliefs. The article "How to Talk to Conservatives About LGBT Rights" uses a storytelling strategy to purposefully create confusion, raise doubt, and encourage young people to embrace an unbiblical view of marriage. The article states,

> Don't win an argument, tell a story. I find stories are a lot more compelling than arguments. So one of the stories I like to tell people is about a gay friend of mine named Mark. Mark was in a religious order and left. He ended up marrying his partner, with whom he's been together for 20 years. One of the things he has done is care for his partner through a long-term serious illness. I often say to people, "Is this not a form of love?" I just ask that question.[1]

A method God created to draw young people to himself is being used to destroy faith. The assumption is that arguments shut Christians down while stories open them up. Young people are more likely to detect a lie when it is presented without disguise, but doctor it up through story and it has the potential to create confusion. The article goes on to state,

> I tend to believe that people are open to experiences. So a closed-minded person who suddenly discovers that his son is gay or her daughter is a lesbian is really forced to look at that differently, because they're confronted with a person instead of a theory, and with an experience instead of a category.[2]

People are open to experiences. Do you believe that? Are your grandchildren ready for this type of argument? Many Christian young people are ill-equipped to counter the power of a good story. Ultimately, this is a test on biblical authority. In this instance, does a young person understand the meaning of marriage through the lens of the Bible or understand the Bible's teaching on marriage through the lens of personal experience?

Satan is a roaring lion who is intent on destroying our grandchildren, and we must recognize the methods he employs so we can counter them. God gave us the power of story to build the faith of future generations in Jesus Christ, and I encourage you to take full advantage of this impactful method.

Key tools

There are a number of creative ideas you could pursue to tell the work of God in your life to your grandchildren. The easiest is to write your experiences in a journal or notebook, or in a document on the computer, and give it to your grandchild in the future. If you are looking for a guide, *The Legacy Journal* by the Christian Grandparenting Network is a helpful resource.

A second idea is to purchase a Bible, highlight key passages you wish to emphasize, and write notes throughout the Bible about God's work in your life. Another option is to share your story in person when the family gathers for a holiday or special life event. One family I know has a different member of the family share their testimony every Christmas; it is a way for the younger generations to hear of the work of the Lord in the lives of different individuals.

Share the Gospel

One of the surprising finds of my PhD dissertation was that less than 25 percent of Christian grandparents are verbally sharing the Gospel with their grandchildren. When asked why, grandparents provided two reasons. First, they did not want to usurp a parent's role. Second, they assumed the Gospel was shared by a grandchild's church, school, or parents.

I understand and appreciate the desire to be sensitive to a parent's responsibility to share the Good News with a child, and am grateful when churches and schools faithfully proclaim the Gospel. However, this should not deter *you* from communicating the Gospel with a grandchild. The presence of Gospel proclamation in one sphere does not eliminate the responsibility of others from sharing it. God places the responsibility of communicating the Gospel on all Christians, and this is true for grandparents with grandchildren.

There are four practical things you can do to share the Gospel confidently and effectively with your grandchild.

1. *See the big picture.* I would be honored to be used by God to personally lead each of my children to faith in Christ. However, let's take a step back and look at the bigger picture. When it comes to the salvation of grandchildren, what matters most: *who* leads a child to Christ, or that a child *has* faith in Christ? Let us be zealous to see our grandchildren come to faith in Jesus, but let us be open to allowing the Spirit to use whom He will, whether that's a parent, grandparent, Sunday school teacher, youth leader, or Christian schoolteacher.

2. *Aim for Gospel repetition.* Children benefit from hearing the Gospel again and again from many sources. Children need to hear the Good News of Christ's life, death, and resurrection at every age and stage. There is no such thing as hearing the Gospel too often, as children are prone to forget the Good News and be captivated by a Gospel replacement. The child who hears the Gospel from parents *and* grandparents is blessed.

3. *Have a conversation.* One way to honor your adult child and ensure that you are not going to do something that catches them off guard is to have a conversation. Communicate your desire to share the Gospel with your grandchild and get the expectations of all parties on the table. If an adult child is territorial about a grandchild's salvation, gently encourage

the adult child to see the bigger picture and to consider the responsibility that God has also given grandparents in the salvation of the next generation. God created parents and grandparents to be discipleship partners raising the next generation for Christ; a conversation helps you work as a team rather than in isolation from one another.

4. *Learn to communicate the Gospel.* Can you communicate the Gospel to a child with clarity and conciseness when an opportunity presents itself? I've found that many adults struggle to communicate the Gospel to a child.

Let's review the Gospel using a four-word outline and explore tools you can use to share the Gospel with your grandchild.

What is the Gospel?

There is no more important message to understand in life than the Gospel. Yet for many Christians, a fog of confusion surrounds the Gospel. If someone says the Gospel is the way of Jesus, the kingdom of God, positive thinking, or compassion toward others, would you be able to explain why each of these explanations is insufficient? The Gospel has been the recipient of massive distortions and oversimplifications. When communicating the Gospel to a grandchild, you should have a threefold aim: (1) clearly understand it, (2) concisely explain it, and (3) confidently proclaim it.

Remembering four words will help you understand, explain, and proclaim the Gospel: God, man, Jesus, and response.[3] These four words summarize the Gospel, which is the Good News because it addresses the most serious problem humans have. R. C. Sproul summarizes this problem by saying, "God is holy and He is just, and I'm not." Here is the Gospel in a nutshell.

God is Creator and He is holy. He is perfect. He has not sinned. He is just; He will not ignore or excuse the sins of others. The

Bible teaches that all humans are accountable to God. He created us; therefore, He can require that we worship Him.

Man has rebelled against God. We have placed ourselves on the throne of life. Romans 1:23 says we have exchanged the glory of God for idols. We are glory thieves, yet God will not share His glory with another. We have fallen short of God's demand for perfection. At the end of life we will stand before a just and holy God and be judged on the basis of our righteousness. We have rebelled against a holy God. That is the bad news.

The good news of the Gospel is that **Jesus** lived a perfect life of righteousness and offered himself as a perfect sacrifice to satisfy the justice of God. God's solution to humanity's sin is the death and resurrection of Jesus. We can be saved from the condemnation our sin deserves through redemption in Jesus (Romans 3:24). The Gospel is news, not advice. It is news that something has happened, and we must respond to it.

A **response** by faith is needed. The great lie of our day is that God forgives everybody, that He is a loving God who sweeps our sins under the carpet and grants forgiveness to those who are good people. The Bible is clear that we are not justified by our works, but by faith alone. Salvation comes "through faith in Jesus Christ" and it is "for all who believe" (Romans 3:22). How is this good news for you? Believe in Jesus Christ and repent of your sins. When you do that, you are declared righteous by God; you are adopted into His family and forgiven of all your sins. God acted in Jesus to save us, and we take hold of that salvation by repentance of sin through faith in Jesus. That's good news. And that is the Gospel.

If you can remember four words—*God, man, Jesus,* and *response*—then you can explain each in further detail. There is nothing more important than sharing the Gospel with our family, so spend time ensuring that you can communicate it clearly and concisely.

Key tools

There are many excellent tools you can use to share the Gospel with a child. Here are a couple of my favorite resources:

The Romans Road explains the Gospel utilizing Romans 3:23; 5:8; 6:23; 10:9–10; and 10:13. All you need is a Bible. If a visual is desired, there are free printable versions available by searching online.

Who Will Be King? There are lots of booklets that can be used to explain the Gospel. I grew up using the Four Spiritual Laws, but for children, one of my favorite Gospel booklets is *Who Will Be King?* I like the booklet because it takes the big concepts of sin and salvation and uses the concrete example of a king to explain them. The booklet is full color, attractive, and affordable. No resource is perfect, and this one has its shortcomings. In an attempt to simplify the Gospel for children, the terminology of the Bible has been paraphrased. You should not shy away from explaining sin, punishment, and the wrath of God. The booklet invites children to say they are sorry to God and ask for forgiveness. My encouragement is to expand upon this paraphrase and invite children to believe and repent.

The *Evangecube* has been used widely in missions across the world. It is a cube, about the size of a Rubik's Cube, that contains pictures to explain the Gospel. The cube is rearranged numerous times while the Gospel is communicated. It is highly interactive and a creative way to share the Gospel. Training workbooks and videos are available online.

There are many more tools to help you share the Gospel, such as the ABCs (admit, believe, confess), the Wordless Book, or a color bracelet. Whether you use a tool or not, you should always be prepared to share the Gospel with a grandchild.

───────────────── **Grand Chat** ─────────────────

1. What opportunities have you had to share wisdom with your grandchildren? What decisions are your children or

grandchildren making and in what ways could you provide wisdom?

2. What has been your experience reading and discussing the Bible with your grandchildren? Have you had any success or do you face any challenges? What resources have you found most helpful?

3. Have you shared your God-stories with your children and grandchildren? How could you incorporate your testimony into a family gathering or an everyday activity with your grandchildren?

4. How have you shared the Gospel with your children or grandchildren? What advice do you have for other grandparents?

12

Intentional Grandparenting: Living in Light of Eternity

BY JOE AND PAM MULVIHILL,
GRANDPARENTS OF SIXTEEN

A common phrase in the Mulvihill family is "Living in light of eternity." This phrase drives us to live our lives in light of God's priorities, to focus our efforts on what matters most, and to invest our time in intentional living. Proverbs 17:6 tells us that "Grandchildren are the crown of the aged," which implies that grandchildren are a cause for great joy and are to be seen as highly valued. Our grandparenting journey has been filled with many fulfilling moments. Along the way we also experienced three unexpected events that have made it more challenging to be an intentional grandparent: the death of our spouses, becoming a blended family, and having a grandchild with special needs. Our challenges may be different from yours, but we trust you will be encouraged by our story and come away with a vision of what it looks like to be an intentional grandparent.

Death

Jane and I (Joe) became grandparents in 2006 and were new to grandparenting when Jane was diagnosed with ALS in December 2007. She passed away on June 11, 2008. I am twice blessed and met Pam in May 2010, and we married in October 2011. Her husband, Jim, had passed away on January 13, 2009, from heart and diabetes complications. The deaths of our spouses were not what we had envisioned for our families; any time a parent is removed, it impacts family dynamics, holiday gatherings, and communication. Intentionality for our family meant that we grieved together, prayed together, and spoke openly about trusting in God's sovereign plan for our family.

Blended Family

We had now become a blended family. I brought four married children and Pam brought two unmarried children into the mix. At the time we met there were four grandchildren. By the time we married, there were seven, so Pam inherited bonus grandchildren, whom she warmly embraced with open arms.

The Mulvihill children were asking the question "So what do we call her? She's not Grandma Mulvihill." The children felt strongly the title was rightly reserved for their mother, Jane, and I (Pam) looked at the *Grandma Mulvihill* title as belonging to Joe's mother. For me it was a generational name. The question of what I would be called remained unanswered as the kids continued to wrestle with this reality. I was initially introduced as Grandpa's friend Pam. Sometime after we married, the families were invited to our home for a gathering. Little Asher, in his larger-than-life style, entered the front door; when I dropped to my knees and held out my arms to welcome him, he rushed into my arms for a hug, exclaiming, "Grammie Pammie!" I was now named. I'm Grammie Pammie, Grandma Pam, Grandma, and the occasional Pam. As life progressed, my two sons married. Since my side of the family didn't have grandchildren until later, the naming of Grandpa Joe is still evolving. We'll turn to the grandchildren again since they have a simple view on life!

Ron Deal, in his book *The Smart Stepfamily*, encourages us to think slow-cooker, not microwave. Anyone with a blended family knows it takes time for relationships to develop. During our dating days, we took part in the monthly Mulvihill gathering that rotated between four homes on the fourth Sunday of the month. These intentional monthly gatherings provided an opportunity for our family to be together and for our blended relationship to grow. As of this writing, we now have sixteen grandchildren, thirteen from Joe's children and three from Pam's children.

Special Needs

We can't say we ever imagined being grandparents to a special-needs grandchild. This reality brought new challenges for us. Our grandson Levi was born in May 2011 with Down syndrome, complex heart disease, and a compromised immune system. During one of his open-heart surgeries he developed chronic respiratory failure, requiring a trach and full ventilation support. Shortly after, we were asked to participate in a training session to learn to care for Levi with a trach. He has been trach-free now for a number of years.

Levi is very active and nonverbal, and his needs are greater than either of us can handle individually, so we attempt to love him, his parents, and siblings as best we can. We express compassion, serve as a pillar of support, and bring hope into their world. We work at being intentional and inclusive so that we are able to further develop our relationship with the entire family. When we have family and holiday gatherings, we adjust the schedule so they can join in for a portion of our time together based on Levi's needs and what he is able to handle. Amy, Levi's mother, on occasion joins Pam for a quilting retreat, and I stay with Jared and the grandchildren for as much of the weekend as possible. I become a second pair of hands to help with Levi and their two younger children. We have found this to be an excellent bonding time with our son and grandchildren.

Intentionality means that we seek to be available and to help as we are able. We pray regularly for Levi and his challenges, as well as for his parents and siblings. We affirm Levi's value and worth and seek to love him unconditionally. As grandparents, we see him as God sees him: that he is a part of God's grand plan in the lives of all he touches, and that he is fearfully and wonderfully made. Levi and his family continue to enrich our lives in new and unexpected ways.

Trust in God

The death of a spouse, blending our families, and having a grandchild with special needs have presented challenges, all of which we have embraced with the confidence that we are walking in God's plan for us. We draw our strength from the trustworthiness of God and His promises in the Bible. God gives us hope that we can do all things through Christ who gives us strength (Philippians 4:13). God tells us that He causes all things to work together for the good of those who love Him and are called according to His purpose (Romans 8:28). God's plan and promises give us assurance that He is working behind the scenes to bring something beautiful out of the difficult things we have walked through. We are encouraged by passages such as Psalm 37:1-9 that remind us not to fret, which frees us to trust in His ways; then we can delight in Him and commit our way unto the Lord. This gives us the strength to persevere through the ups and downs we've experienced.

One of our favorite sayings is "Don't wait for the storm to pass, but learn to dance in the rain." Are you learning to dance with Christ as your hope and strength in the midst of the storms of life? If you are, that's tremendous. We encourage you to model this truth to your grandchildren as God gives you the opportunity. If you are struggling with a difficult family situation, then our encouragement is to trust in the Lord and His promises.

We Have Kingdom Work to Do

Pam and I gained greater clarity about grandparenting after attending a regional grandparenting conference that Josh organized, where God expanded our understanding of our role and calling as grandparents through him and the other presenters. We came away realizing we needed to be more intentional with our grandchildren. We are not off the hook and shouldn't coast along. We have family and kingdom work to do. We need to roll up our sleeves and stay purposely engaged, and that means all the way to the grave. As long as we are living, this calling never ends.

There tends to be a predominant view that grandparents can sit back, relax, and travel. "We've raised our kids, now it's your turn to raise yours, so here's the baton. Have fun!" We still seek to model a Christian lifestyle, spend time with our grandchildren here and there, have fun, play games, and go on outings, but ultimately send them home where the real work of forming them rests with their parents. We might even spoil them a bit before sending them home. Grandparents often believe they are off the hook in shaping grandchildren and not responsible for how they turn out.

Jane and I were very intentional in raising our children to be well-rounded in the major areas of life: physical, emotional, social, spiritual, and financial. Each of these major categories had numerous sub-points we worked on with each of them at the appropriate ages from birth through college graduation as we sought to prepare them for independence. With our children raised and married, we are ushered into the grandparenting chapter of life.

Out of this previous practice with our children, Pam and I now bring intentionality to our role as grandparents in three areas: leaving a heritage, building a legacy, and modeling authentic Christian living.

Leaving a Heritage

Scripture reminds us that "A good man leaves an inheritance to his children's children" (Proverbs 13:22). What do we want to leave our grandchildren when we are gone? What kind of deposits do we want to make in their lives? Pam and I have thought about these questions, and we encourage you to do the same. To get you started, here are five areas we highly value:

- Most important, we want *to leave them with the Gospel.* We want them to adopt the faith in Christ we profess and one day own it for themselves.
- Because we *value living in light of eternity*, our hope is that they will make life choices that reflect this priority. One of the joys of being a grandparent is helping our children and grandchildren make wise, God-honoring decisions.
- We want *to pass on a good family name*, one they can be proud of and that can serve to motivate them to stay faithful in living for Christ all the days of their lives.
- Jane and I *valued Christian education* and made this investment in our children's lives all the way through college. In light of this value, now Pam and I have made an investment for a number of years to the Christian school where three of our grandchildren now attend. We also have begun a small fund for each of our grandchildren's college education.
- We are working on *a written history of what life was like for us* when growing up so that history does not become lost after we are no longer around.

166

―――――――――――――――― **Building a Legacy** ――――――――――

Psalm 78:4-7 instructs grandparents to tell and to teach future generations about God, and has encouraged us to ask the following questions: What do we want to build during our lifetime that generations coming after us will be inspired by and are moved by God to continue building upon? What do we want them to know about us? How do we want to be remembered at our Celebration Service when this life has come to an end? Thinking about these questions has helped us live more intentionally as grandparents, and we encourage you to think about them as well. Here are a few of the ways that we want to build a legacy:

- We want to *be known as a Christ follower*. We want them to know of our coming to faith in Christ and provide them with a written copy of our faith story so they can take it forward with them and share with future generations.

- We want them to know *we have taken the Great Commission of Christ seriously*, His command to make disciples of all nations, by going and sharing the Gospel with others, by leading some to faith in Christ, and by baptizing and teaching them to observe His commands. We want them to know we chose to invest the best years of our lives by way of our time, our talents, and our vocational calling to nearly four decades of full-time Christian service with Campus Crusade for Christ; that we ordered our lives in line with His Great Commission; that we walked by faith, not by sight; and that we literally trusted in His provision for our daily needs. He proved himself trustworthy as we did our part in growing daily and following after Him, and He did His part in providing for us as a faith-supported mission.

- We want to be *known as a family that loved, cared for, prayed for, and supported one another*. That our children, grandchildren, and beyond can take pride in the fact that they are our descendants.

- We *pray for our grandchildren regularly*. We pray each of them will come to faith in Christ at an early age, choose to follow Christ as the Lord of their lives, desire to grow in their walk of faith in Him, desire to make Him known to others, get engaged in His Great Commission, and if it is God's will for them to marry one day, that their future spouse will have the same things true about them as we pray for our grandchildren.

- We *memorize Scripture with any of our grandchildren* who want to practice this spiritual discipline together.

- We make it a point to *participate in Grandparent's Day* at our grandchildren's school, as well as other school and athletic events throughout the year.

- We want to be *known as disciple-makers*. We want to see it begin with our own children and see them pass on the faith to their children and from our grandchildren to their children (our great-grandchildren), and on to future generations. We want to look back on life and see our children and grandchildren following Christ and making disciples of their children (2 Timothy 2:2). If it doesn't work at home, we have no business exporting it to others.

- We focus on *giving gifts of time rather than things*. A number of our children tell us their kids are already drowning in things. We believe time builds better memories with our grandchildren than toys do. How does a child spell love? T-I-M-E. We are fortunate to have fourteen of the sixteen living nearby. Long-distance grandparenting to out-of-state grandchildren presents its own set of challenges. With intentionality, we are able to somewhat bridge that gap with planned travel and face-to-face communications with social media and technology options, such as FaceTime. We've had sleepovers, including a tent in the backyard, dates for lunch, tea with a granddaughter and her favorite doll, baking and cooking together, snow sliding, hiking in the woods, fishing, and game time. We purchased a membership to the Science Museum of Minnesota, where we take the grandchildren periodically and discuss what we observed and how it's tied into God's majesty. Interactions at grandparent camp and granddad-and-lad camp have included canoeing, target practice with BB guns, camp games, campfires, various tournaments, devotions together, and chapel time with the Christian theme running throughout.

- We put together a *small photo book for each of the grandchildren*. Each book contains photos of time we spent together with them on numerous occasions from birth up to the year we assembled the book. Over time we want to come back and update them with new moments and photos from where we left off with each of them—a living, breathing documentation of our presence in each of their lives, memory makers, as vehicles in building that legacy.

- *We plan outings* further out than we initially preferred because we've learned that busy lives for both our grandchildren and ourselves require early planning. We have discovered it's easier to plan early rather than trying to squeeze something in. We appreciate spontaneous activities and remain hopeful that our intentionality will serve to fuel these ongoing relationships. We need to be willing to adjust and engage the grandchildren as they grow and mature to stay connected.

Modeling Authentic Christian Living

Grandparenting is more than what we do. It begins with who we are as followers of Christ (see Colossians 3:1-17). What does this look like for us?

- *Be yourself; don't try to be someone you're not.* God has made you a certain way, with certain talents, gifts, skills, and desires. Learn and recognize them for what they are and be authentic. We are real, open, and honest with our grandchildren. If we've blown it with them in the past, we ask for their forgiveness.

- We want to be known as *people of honorable Christian character*; intentionally striving so that our walk matches our talk, that we live out the heart of Christ in our family and beyond, that we don't bring shame to the name of Christ, and that we prove faithful throughout life to the cause of Christ.

- One of the things Jane and I modeled with our kids was to take *two to three planning weekends a year.* Pam and I make an investment in our children's marriages so they can do the same, with the benefit that we get to spend concentrated time with our grandchildren. Our children get away alone together to step back, relax, reconnect, have fun, plan, evaluate, and pray together over their marriage, family, and vocational calling. Any time we have the grandchildren for bedtime, we make it a practice to do something with them for a bedtime devotional and prayer together.

Conclusion

If God is all knowing, all powerful, and supreme over all things, and we believe He is, then none of your grandparenting challenges take Him by surprise. God was aware of your specific grandparent situation and your unique challenges in eternity past, before the foundation of time, and has preordained it to come to pass. Will you by faith thank Him for it and trust in His goodness? Our faith in Him is not a blind leap of faith but a faith based on the substance of the trustworthiness of God and His Word, changed lives, historical, archeological, scientific, and philosophical evidence. If you would like to talk further about any of these evidences, we would welcome the opportunity. You may contact us at jmpm dancing@gmail.com.

We have a high and holy calling from God to be intentional with each of the grandchildren He blesses us with and to invest in each of them based on their age. We implore you as grandparents to finish strong and well, stay the course all the way to the end, that it may be said of you, "Well done, good and faithful servant."

PART 4

STRENGTHENING RELATIONSHIPS

13

Developing Strong Relationships
The Foundation for Family Discipleship

I regularly ask grandparents what they love most about being a grandparent, and Mary's response is common: "What I like the most about being a grandparent is the absolute unconditional love between us. The joy in their hugs and smiles and the leaping into our arms, the bolt out the door and sprint down the driveway as soon as they see our car. The quiet snuggles reading a story or watching a movie. The constant 'Watch me, Nana!' and 'Look what I can do!' To be a grandparent is joy, joy, joy deep in my heart!"

Grandparenting is a great source of joy. It can also be a source of pain. Almost always, the amount of joy or pain has a direct correlation to the state of the relationship between family members. This section will help you develop and maintain strong family relationships so that you have the greatest potential to disciple future generations.

The primary point of this entire section is this: *A strong relationship is the foundation by which the Gospel can be transmitted and discipleship between the generations can occur.*

Strong relationships are important for three reasons. First, our family relationships are a reflection of Christ to others. They are a billboard that communicates the Gospel to a watching world. Christians are to be known by their love, and that includes our families. Second, strong relationships reinforce the truth of Scripture and become a strong apologetic to convince children and grandchildren that Christianity is true. If we say we love Jesus but do not act like Him in our family relationships by allowing the relational principles of Scripture to guide us, this hypocrisy may drive children away from Christ. It is disastrous if our love for God does not shape how we love others in our home. Third, strong relationships are important because they are a good gift from God to be joyfully received and faithfully stewarded. If relationships with family are filled with conflict and unpleasant experiences, we tend to avoid one another, which negatively impacts intimacy. On the other hand, we gravitate toward positive experiences, good memories, and happy relationships.

The Bible references strong relationships with family by stating, "He will turn the hearts of fathers to their children and the hearts of children to their fathers" (Malachi 4:6). God's desire is a strong heart connection between family members, for it is then that the good news of the Gospel can be received and the truths of Scripture embraced. How do you develop a strong relationship with your family? Here are six ways.

View Grandchildren as a Blessing

Do you remember what you felt when you learned that you would be a grandparent? Were you enthusiastic or ambivalent? Excited or anxious? Motivated or mad? Did you see your new grandchild as a blessing or a burden?

I don't ask those questions flippantly, as I've experienced the entire spectrum with Christian grandparents. Your attitude about being a grandparent reveals much about your heart and what you believe about grandparenting. But your attitude toward grandparenting *should* reflect God's attitude. And what is God's attitude toward grandparenting?

The Bible tells us that it is a blessing to *know* your grandchildren. "May you see your children's children!" (Psalm 128:6). The ministry of grandparenting is to be received as a blessing, not rejected as a burden. The grandparent who has a poor attitude toward grandparenthood in general or a grandchild specifically is at odds with God's plan.

Every grandchild is created in the image of God and is therefore His sovereign plan for your life. Every grandchild is to be highly valued regardless of gender, race, health, or personality. Every grandchild is to be received with love and embraced as God's good design for your life.

Grandchildren are a blessing. Do you believe that? Or do you resent the cost and commitment of grandparenting? By nature, grandparenting requires sacrifice. It asks us to die to ourselves and our wants. Think for a moment about the sacrifices grandparenting has required of you. What was your attitude? What was your response? Maybe the birth of a grandchild has required that you alter your plan, brought about a change in family dynamics, or led to expectations and reprioritizations that you don't like.

If you've ever wished a grandchild wasn't born or that you never became a grandparent, you're not alone. I've met many grandparents who won't verbally admit that they view a grandchild as a burden, but harbor these feelings in their heart.

If you struggle to receive a grandchild as a blessing, what do you do? First, pray that God would soften your heart and change your attitude. Ask God to give you His love for a grandchild and pray this prayer again and again. I've found that when I pray for someone, it is hard to stay disappointed or upset with them.

Second, you must release your plans to the Lord and choose to trust God's sovereign plan even when life turns out differently than envisioned. The Bible reminds us, "The heart of man plans his way, but the Lord establishes his steps" (Proverbs 16:9). Understanding

God's sovereignty is foundational to being joyful despite the circumstances. I never envisioned my children's grandmothers dying in their fifties, but we have embraced God's good plan for our family and trust that the King of Kings has a purpose for everything He does in our lives.

Third, we must allow the Bible to shape our view of grandchildren. The Bible tells us that it is a blessing to *have* grandchildren. "Grandchildren are a crown of the aged" (Proverbs 17:6). That significant statement speaks to the incredible value of grandchildren. Interestingly, it is not wealth, health, career accomplishments, or social status that the Bible says is the crowning achievement of your life. That honor goes to grandchildren.

A crown bestows honor and represents a high position in life unmatched through any other source. Grandchildren are the real crown of life—not square footage, exotic vacations, strong portfolios, or living in a warm climate. Your attitude and actions should reflect the value given to grandchildren by God in Scripture.

Aim for the Heart

Popular logic goes something like this: "Remove children from bad influences and they will make good choices." There is some truth to this statement, but there is also the danger of misapplication. As a parent of five children, I am very intentional about what my children are exposed to. I do not want them around impurity. Yet even from a young age, before my children were a year old, they innately knew how to disobey.

How do children learn to do what is wrong? Mark 7:21–23 answers this question: "For from within, out of the heart of man, come evil thoughts. . . . All these evil things come from within, and they defile a person."

The Bible teaches that all humanity, including your grandchild, is naturally inclined to do what is evil; it comes from within a person. Our wickedness is often believed to result from bad example, bad company, specific temptations, or from the devil himself. These influences are significant and should not be ignored, as they can strongly impact behavior, but they should not be thought of as the primary cause for wrong choices. It must not be forgotten that every person carries within themselves a fountain of wickedness. Your grandchildren need none of the aforementioned causes because the seed of sin exists in their heart.

We ought to remember this in the training and discipleship of our grandchildren. In all our grandparenting we must never forget that the seeds of all mischief and wickedness are in the heart of a grandchild. It is not enough to try to control a child's environment and shield him from every outward evil (although this should be part of our strategy). Children carry within them a heart ready for sin, and until the heart is changed, children are not safe. The task of parenting and grandparenting is not merely training a child to behave properly, but addressing the core sinfulness of the heart. An engagement with the root cause of human sinfulness should be the goal (Romans 3:23; 6:23).

How thankful we ought to be for the Gospel. Through Jesus' atoning death on the cross, God provided a way to pay for all our wickedness and to make our heart pure. As shepherds to children, our highest calling is to work with God to see that children know and embrace the Gospel. Grandparents, in partnership with parents, should be diligent to shield children from negative influences, but we should not see this action as an end in itself. Children need a new heart, and that is only possible through faith in Jesus Christ. Aim for the heart and your grandchild's conversion; keep the Gospel of Jesus at the center of all you do. This is the heart of grandparenting.

Protect Your Marriage

My grandparents were married for sixty-seven years. That is an incredible accomplishment and an amazing gift to my family. It is also a declining reality for older couples.

There's a tendency to believe that divorce is something that happens to young couples, but there is a growing trend called "gray divorce": once children grow up and move away, older couples often see no reason to continue a difficult marriage. About one in four divorces now occur among couples over fifty, and 15 percent of Americans over fifty are divorced.[1]

One of the strongest deterrents for divorce is found in Malachi 2:15: "Did he not make them one [referring to marriage], with a portion of the Spirit in their union? And what was the one God seeking? Godly offspring. So guard yourselves in your spirit, and let none of you be faithless to the wife of your youth."

Marriage is the artery that carries the Gospel to children and grandchildren; in Malachi's words, one of its purposes is to produce godly offspring. Severing the artery impacts the delivery of the Gospel, meaning that divorce may produce *ungodly* offspring.

Sometimes when I'm counseling a couple considering divorce I ask them, "Would you get a divorce if you knew it meant that your child or grandchild was going to reject Jesus and spend eternity without Him?" That's a heavy question. I don't ask it lightly. The Bible teaches that divorce impacts the faith of future generations. That is meant to motivate us to lifelong faithfulness.

Research echoes what the Bible teaches; divorce impacts children spiritually and increases the odds that children will walk away from Christ. One study found that children of divorced homes are 12 percent more likely to be nonreligious.[2] The argument that divorce is good for children and grandchildren is simply not true.

If you want to raise children and grandchildren who love Jesus, then do everything possible to avoid divorce. The predominant view among conservative evangelical Christians is that the Bible allows for divorce due to unrepentant adultery and abandonment by a Gospel-rejecting spouse. In such cases, much discernment and wise Christian counsel is needed. If you find yourself in a difficult marriage, I encourage you to do everything you can to fight for your marriage.

Marriage is the center of all family relationships. When marriage is strong, family is strong. When a marriage struggles, all else struggles, including the transmission of faith. Marital problems always spill into other areas of life, so work to protect your marriage.

Prioritize Family First

A key discipleship principle from the Bible is *family first*. God created a discipleship progression in Scripture that begins with your heart, moves to the home, and extends outward. Notice the family-first mentality of Acts 2:39: "For the promise is for you and for your children, and for all who are far off." The biblical pattern encourages us to prioritize the discipleship of family over others.

Jesus commands His followers to make disciples of all nations, which is to begin in our city and extend to the rest of the world (Matthew 28:18–20). Before we go beyond the walls of our own home to share the Gospel with others, we must begin the work of making disciples of our own children and grandchildren. If we go to our neighbors and nations but neglect our own family, we have skipped a critical step. Healthy discipleship includes a Gospel concern for everyone in our sphere and is not exclusive. However, to neglect one's family for any reason is not healthy or praiseworthy.

"I need to reprioritize who I'm discipling," said a grandmother who heard me speak on discipling the family. "I've been mentoring young mothers at my church, but not my own children. I've decided to reduce the number of young mothers I'm mentoring so I can invest in my own family." While it is always hard to say no to fruitful ministry opportunities, I believe this was a good and God-honoring choice that reflects the pattern of Scripture for disciple-making.

I encourage you to follow God's discipleship progression with your family. God expects disciple-making to begin at home, then move across the street, and then around the world. The problem is that many Christians either are not intentionally discipling their family or are heavily investing in neighbors and nations, yet neglecting to make disciples of their own family.

Offer Help

Today's parents feel overwhelmed; the *Huffington Post* declared that overwhelmed parents are so common that it is a "national crisis."[3] Parents are overworked, family life is overscheduled, and your adult children often feel overwhelmed. The result is high levels of stress that lead to irritability, anxiety, depression, and insomnia.

Parents believe it is more difficult to raise children today than in the past.[4] What is it that makes parenting difficult today? According to a Barna study, here are the top nine factors: technology/social media, the world is more dangerous, lack of a common morality, financial factors, bullying at school, high academic pressure, my (or spouse's) work is more demanding, living far away from family, an exposure to cultural/religious diversity.

Whether parenting is more difficult today is debatable. Regardless, today's parents often struggle under the weight of child-rearing and the endless tasks that come with parenting. Here are a couple of examples from parents:

> Now that I am back to work full time, I get up at 5:00 a.m. to get the kids' lunches ready. I often find myself doing laundry at 10:00 p.m. Last week I was picking up groceries at the supermarket at 11:00 p.m., and my stomach is churning while driving to the day care center because I don't want to be charged the late pick-up fee. I'm so exhausted at night when I go to bed, I can hardly talk to my husband, much less make love with him. I don't like living this way, but I'm not seeing a way out.[5]

> When it comes to parenting, our work is never done. Things shout at us from every direction, making it easy to get perpetually stuck

in doing mode. *Help Sammy with his spelling words! Take the splinter out of Shannon's finger! Do the dishes . . . feed the dog . . . sign the permission slip . . . get the boys in their bath . . . !*[6]

It doesn't matter what causes the overwhelm. Sometimes it can be a culmination of little stressors—orange peels left on the floor, peanut butter on the stairs, sassing back by the eight year old, kids that don't want to go to bed, bills piling on the counter—or it can be just that life is deciding that at this moment it's simply going to be hard. Money stuff. Relationship issues. Sickness. Death. Kid issues.[7]

Parents aren't just overwhelmed by endless tasks, they are also overwhelmed by the volume of opinions about how to parent. Facebook feeds are full of opinions about nutrition, education, health care, and athletics. Academic research presents compelling arguments from different perspectives on media consumption, brain development, vaccinations, and a long list of other topics parents should consider. Family and friends offer varied philosophical approaches with strong views about sleep training, self-esteem, positive reinforcement, and discipline. Parents, especially those not well grounded in God's Word, struggle to gain clarity, lack child-rearing confidence, and are unsure how to raise children to treasure Christ.

Parents today experience these challenges, and God has created grandparents to help. Here are four practical ways you can help your adult child:

- *Point them to the Bible.* Parents are increasingly taking their parenting cues from sources other than the Bible. The more Scripture informs what your children do and how they do it, the more God can transform their heart and home.
- *Don't pile on the guilt.* Many parents silently wonder if they are cut out to parent. Remind your adult child that God is sovereign and chose your child to be the exact parent for that exact child. Difficult situations do not define us, God does.

- *Give courage to face the day.* Sometimes all an adult child needs to hear is that you believe in them and that they can make it. If you want to give your adult child a big boost, tell them you love them and are proud of them. Encourage your child to do the next thing that needs to be done and take it one step at a time.
- *Ask how you can help.* Parents often need help with day-to-day tasks of managing a home, such as cleaning the house, preparing a meal, doing the laundry, mowing the lawn, home repair, or a break from children. If your adult child does not accept your offer, that's okay; offer again at a later time.

Parents aren't just overwhelmed by the daily tasks of raising children and running a family. Many are also overwhelmed, or at least unsure, about how to raise their children to love and follow Jesus. Parents have quiet fears about messing up their child and are unsure what to do. I was reminded of this fact when I was a family pastor. A guest pastor presented many of the cultural challenges for young people today and his diagnosis was excellent. However, he provided few solutions, and the result was a long line of alarmed parents. One parent said to me, "I have no idea what to do. I'm paralyzed with fear. I don't want to repeat my parents' mistakes. I know I should be doing something, but I don't know what that is. So I haven't done anything to help my children grow in their faith."

Grandparents have a golden opportunity. There will be times when your adult children feel overwhelmed by life and unsure of how to parent. God created you to point your children to Him and to share the weight of raising the next generation to know Him.

Develop a Personal Relationship with Every Family Member

You should make it a priority to *personally* develop a strong relationship with each child, son- or daughter-in-law, and grandchild. I emphasize the word *personally* because I've observed that many grandparents, particularly grandfathers, have a relationship with family primarily through their spouse. It is not uncommon for the grandmother to be the one who talks on the phone, remembers birthdays, purchases gifts, initiates gatherings, and makes family a priority. Grandfathers contribute, but on a much smaller scale.

Take this test. Imagine that your spouse died and you were 100 percent responsible for maintaining relationships with your children and grandchildren. How heavily do you rely on your spouse to maintain a relationship with each family member? If it's an abundant amount, make it a priority to personally invest in developing stronger relationships.

A strong relationship with children and grandchildren is essential in order to disciple them. These six areas of attitude, aim, marriage, family first, help, and a personal relationship each have the potential to strengthen relationships in your family.

Grand Chat

1. What was your response when you learned you were going to be a grandparent?
2. Read and discuss Psalm 128:6. What is your view of grandchildren—a blessing or a burden? What sacrifices has grandparenting required of you and how have you responded?
3. Read Proverbs 17:6. What does it mean that grandchildren are a crown of the aged?
4. Read Malachi 2:15. According to this verse, what is one reason to avoid divorce? Do you have any advice to share with others regarding how to develop and maintain a healthy marriage?
5. When have your children felt overwhelmed with parenting or life in general? In what ways have you offered to help them?
6. What is the state of your relationship with each of your children and grandchildren?

14

Factors That Impact Relationships

Three Ways to Increase Intimacy

Have you wondered why some grandparents have close relationships with grandchildren and others do not? Some factors are beyond our control, but others are not. Researchers have studied the factors that lead to intimate relationships between grandparents and grandchildren, and found three themes emerged: physical proximity, frequency of contact, and quality of relationship.[1]

Physical Proximity

The single most important factor that determines a grandparent's involvement with family is geographic distance. The closer grandparents live to grandchildren, the greater the likelihood of interaction between grandparent and grandchild, which leads to a deeper relationship. Grandparents who live a long distance geographically from family can still have meaningful relationships with children and grandchildren, but it will require two things: intentionality and technology. Although there is no substitute for face-to-face interaction, technology has made it possible to develop a relationship with a grandchild from a distance. If you are a slow adopter, my encouragement is to embrace technology to use it to connect with family. Make it a priority to communicate weekly, be intentional about planning face-to-face family gatherings, and be willing to travel if needed.

Here are two examples of grandparents intentionally navigating the proximity challenge. Janet and her husband purposefully decided to move closer to family. Janet told me,

> It's been a huge difference. Before, they either lived in Florida or Virginia. So we maybe got to see them twice a year, at most, for a week or two. At first the kids were babies, so it took a while for them to really know who we were. Now they know who Grammie and Grandpa are, and they are older, so the relationship is totally different. They are very familiar with us.

Mike and Debbie have children who live in different states and have made it a priority to travel and spend time with each child's family.

> We pursue a relationship by going to see them. They visit us as well, but we go to see our kids as much as we can. We are often visitors in their home. Sometimes we bring the motor home and spend two or three weeks with them. We live with them as part of the family and then we would go back home and we would look forward to the next visit. We go there as often or more as they come here. I think grandparents are more free to go than the parents are.

Frequency of Contact

Research also reveals that the quality of a grandparent and grandchild relationship is based on the frequency of interaction. Studies have revealed that over half of grandparents interact with grandchildren once a month or less.[2] Not surprisingly, it is difficult to develop a deep and intimate relationship with limited contact.

A wise grandmother stated to me, "I have a mantra. I've had it for many years. This idea of spending quality time is a myth. What kids need is a lot of quantity time. And we tried to do that. . . . You need to spend huge quantities of quality time with your kids and grandkids if you want them to be willing to have a relationship with you. They've got to know that you care."

Whether you live close or far from family, Carolyn believes the smartphone is an essential grandparenting tool:

> We get pictures that we respond to. We do FaceTime. Our grandson is taking piano lessons, and we were able to hear his first performance, "Ode to Joy." They put it on the iPhone and sent it to us. Yesterday we received a picture from our other grandson who made a *Star Wars* ship out of Legos. We had an opportunity to respond back and encourage him and *ooh* and *aah* about how creative he is. The day before I had gotten a text saying he had just thrown up all over the couch, so I was able to send a text back saying, "I'm so sorry you don't feel well." He knew I was praying for him and hoping he would get better.

How often do you interact with each grandchild? If your interaction is infrequent, a simple way to increase your impact is to increase your frequency of interaction. Texting, letter writing, phone calls, and face-to-face visits are all tools grandparents can use to increase interaction. What can you do to increase your frequency of contact?

Quality of Relationship

Research has revealed that the quality of your relationship with your grandchild's parents, particularly their mother, is one of the most important factors that influences the quality of relationship between grandparent and grandchild.

Parents are the gatekeepers of their children, granting or restricting access. Intimacy with adult children paves the way for intimacy with grandchildren. Not surprisingly, a strained relationship with adult children impacts your opportunity and ability to interact with your grandchildren. One of the best ways you can influence your grandchildren, and increase the amount of time spent with them, is to develop and maintain a strong relationship with your adult child and their spouse. Here are three ways you can do that.

- *Pay attention to your words.* Ephesians 4:29 is your guide regarding how to talk about your adult children to your grandchildren: "Let no corrupting talk come out of your mouths, but only such as is good for building up, as fits the occasion, that it may give grace to those who hear." Your talk is to build up, not corrupt your adult child's authority and credibility. Pay careful attention to the questions you ask, the sarcastic remarks, under-the breath-comments, or complaining statements that undermine a parent.

- *Pay attention to your feelings.* Your feelings about adult children are often transmitted to grandchildren. If negative perceptions or feelings find their way back to an adult child, the impact on a relationship is almost always negative.

- *Pay attention to your expectations.* We all have a set of role assumptions for one another. Grandparents expect frequent contact with grandchildren and gratitude from family members. Mothers expect non-interfering support with the day-to-day pressures of life and parenting. Grandchildren expect grandparents to share history and give gifts. Relationship satisfaction is directly connected to identifying and delivering on the expectations of others. Your job is to go one step further. Talk about expectations, work to shape the expectations, and then do your best to deliver on them.

If you want a closer relationship with a grandchild, consider addressing one or more of these factors. Increased time and attention provides greater opportunity for you to develop a deep relationship with family.

Grand Chat

1. If your grandchildren live at a distance, how have you developed and maintained a close relationship?
2. How have you used technology to maintain communication with your family?
3. What have been your greatest communication challenges and successes?
4. What kinds of adjustments or changes could you make related to physical proximity, frequency of contact, and quality of relationship to increase relational intimacy?

15

Gospel-Shaped Grandparenting

Five Statements That Can Transform Your Family

God calls grandparents to be disciple-makers of future generations by passing on a heritage of faith in Jesus. For many grandparents, the combination of biblical direction plus discipleship tools is all that is needed to engage with family. For others, there are barriers or obstacles that make the implementation of family discipleship difficult. I call it *messy grandparenting*.

Messy grandparenting exists because we live in a sinful world. In an ideal world, all of our children love Jesus, marry Christian spouses who are easy to get along with, raise children who follow Christ, and maintain an intimate relationship with us. In a sinful world, there are disappointments, brokenness, and difficult family situations that prevent or impede family discipleship. Maybe you're experiencing deep sadness, a lot of hurt, relational tensions, grandparenting restrictions, adult prodigals, or divorce, and wonder what to do.

What happens when parenting or grandparenting doesn't go according to plan? What happens when problems arise and we find ourselves in the midst of a challenging family situation? God's Word provides general guidelines that we can apply to our relationships. That's what this chapter is going to address.

Two Challenges

The Mulvihill family has experienced two significant challenges, and by God's grace we saw that He took what was difficult and redeemed it for good. The first challenge came in 2008 when my mother died from ALS. Mothers are the relational hub of the family, and when you take them out of the mix it dramatically alters family dynamics such as the frequency of communication, holiday traditions, and how a family interacts. The Mulvihill family had to relearn how to function without Mom in the mix. It took time, patience, and lots of communication. In addition, my children never knew their grandmother personally, and Jen and I no longer had my mom's godly parenting wisdom in our life.

The second challenge came in 2014 when my mother-in-law died from brain cancer. Debbie's death was a big blow to our family. When some grandparents die, their impact is minimal and it doesn't change anything tangible for their grandchildren. But Debbie grandparented in a way that left a void after she died because of the meaningful place she had in our lives.

Grandparents are partners with parents, working toward the same goal of raising future generations in the Lord. Jen and I found it challenging when both grandmothers were no longer alive. We lost partners in the Gospel as well as family support. Due to the absence of biological grandmothers in my children's life, I can confirm what the Bible teaches: grandparents matter. A family with no grandmothers was not how we envisioned our future, and it required that we look to Scripture and to the Gospel to determine how to navigate our new and unexpected reality.

God, in His goodness, gave my children a new grandmother. In 2011 I had the privilege of officiating my dad's wedding to Pam, a wonderful Christian woman. My children call her Grammie Pammie, and she is a gift to our family. We love Pam and are grateful for her godly influence in our lives. Being a blended family is not without its challenges, but by God's grace there is much laughter when we get together, and we continue to grow in our love for one another.

When brokenness touches our family we naturally ask questions about how to navigate the challenges. This is where the Gospel comes into play. If the Gospel doesn't answer our grandparenting problem, then we don't fully understand the Gospel. The Gospel is central for Christians and the whole of Christianity. Everything about grandparenting should find its place in relation to the Gospel.

How does the Gospel impact how you live on a daily basis as a grandparent? I'm going to answer that question with five statements that can transform your family:

I Love You

God the Father provided an example of fatherly love when He announced of Jesus, "This is my Son, whom I love; with him I am well pleased" (Matthew 3:17 NIV). When was the last time you verbally told each family member you loved him or her? When was the last time you told an adult child you were proud of her or that he was doing a good job parenting? No one gets tired of hearing the words "I love you" or "Well done." Every adult child and grandchild I've met benefits from being told they are loved. Some children desperately want to hear those words come out of a parent's mouth.

A parent's love, even for an adult child, is a powerful force. Here are three examples from Scripture: the love of a father helped bring the prodigal son home; the love of a mother-in-law helped the widow Ruth through a period of suffering; the love of Timothy's grandmother Lois helped Eunice raise a God-fearing son. Love invites rebellious children home, is a refuge in time of need, and is the first line of family defense.

If we follow the pattern of the Gospel, we love with no strings attached and no expectation that it will be reciprocated. Gospel-shaped grandparenting means that we love first and are willing to initiate. God loved us when we were not lovely, and He sought us out when we were in active rebellion against Him. The pattern of Scripture that God calls us to in our relationships is unconditional and sacrificial love.

Gospel love means that we treat everyone like they are an image-bearer of God. Genesis 1:27 is our road map. All grandchildren, including those with special needs, a difficult personality, or behavior challenges, have incredible value not because of what they do but because they are made by God. As a grandparent you can be a safe place and a loving presence in a world that is cruel and cold. In-laws or adopted grandchildren are not to be treated as second-class citizens. They should be loved as much as biological children and grandchildren. Gospel love results in committed faithfulness and is our guide regarding how we love our family.

Gospel love is costly. It requires sacrifice. It invests even when it hurts. Sacrificial love means that if your family is in need, you are the first to offer support. God expects you to be the first to help your family (1 Timothy 5:8). How much should you help your family? Gospel love is generous. Jesus didn't give 10 percent of His blood; He gave his whole life. If we live by the law, we give a certain amount and then believe we are done. If we live by the Gospel, we give freely based on need without expectation of repayment. Of course, discernment is needed. The Bible tells us that if we have a lazy family member who does not work, financial support may hinder his need or desire to do so (2 Thessalonians 3:10; Proverbs 6:6–11).

Gospel love is unconditional. Do you have a family member who is difficult to love? If so, God provides wisdom in the Bible to help you navigate challenging family relationships, such as to guard your tongue, provide a gentle answer, love your enemy, and look at the speck in your own eye. Gospel love is patient and kind as well as gracious and caring (1 Corinthians 13:4–7). There are many helpful biblical principles we could explore and apply to our family relationships. Rather than list individual passages, I want to remind you of God's overall pattern. God loved us while we were yet sinners, and we should do the same for family members who are difficult to love or who are living in rebellion to God.

A grandfather approached me with tears in his eyes and said, "My twenty-four-year-old grandson Wyatt just announced he doesn't believe in Christianity. What do I do? What do I say when he comes over? It's going to be awkward." Here is what I told this grandfather and how I helped him apply the Gospel to this situation.

- Wyatt still needs to know that he is loved. Saying "I love you" does not mean you agree with or approve of his actions. Maintaining the relationship is important because relationships are the artery that deliver the Gospel.

- Love meets people where they are at, not where they should be. Don't alienate a grandchild by making an issue over lifestyle choices.

- Invite him to your home for dinner. Jesus dined with sinners and you can too.

- Ephesians 4:29 is your guide regarding how to talk. In general, it is good to say less and pray more. Your words should be seasoned with love.

- Don't talk to a grandchild as if everything is fine when it isn't. The challenge is to balance grace and truth in a loving way.

- One of the marks of love is self-control. You are going to need self-control in conversation and over social media. Watch your social media conduct. Don't get rattled by a grandchild's posts.

Every challenge is distinct and complex, yet they are all addressed through the sufficiency of Scripture. God provides clear instructions in the Bible on how we are to respond to sinful behavior, and models of how to love a prodigal child for us to imitate.

Please Forgive Me. I Forgive You.

Are you prepared to navigate sin in family relationships? What happens when your adult child does something that hurts you? How about when it is repetitive and there is no repentance? The Gospel does not call us to fix others; it calls us to forgive others.

Many family relationships are negatively affected by an unbiblical response to offenses or hurts. An attitude of grace and willingness to forgive is essential to maintaining strong family relationships.

Our motivation to forgive is not due to others' actions or attitudes. Forgiveness is patterned after what God has done for us. Biblical principles of forgiveness include the following:

- *Forgiveness is modeled after God's love.* "Be kind and compassionate to one another, forgiving one another, just as in Christ God forgave you" (Ephesians 4:32 NIV).
- *Forgiveness cancels a debt.* We choose not to hold a sin against someone. Unforgiveness is often motivated by the desire that the offending person work to pay for their sin. Many relationships are ruined when forgiveness is withheld until someone feels payment or punishment has been achieved.
- *Forgiveness is a choice.* Mark 11:25 tells us, "Whenever you stand praying, forgive, if you have anything against anyone, so that your Father also who is in heaven may forgive you your trespasses."
- *Forgiveness is an ongoing process.* It takes time to heal. Every time we remember the offense, we need to continue to forgive and resist the sinful desire for revenge.

- *Forgiveness makes a promise.* I will not talk about the offense again with others, or hold it against you, and I will not purposefully think about it.
- *Forgiveness does not mean a relationship is restored.* It means an offense is released. Reconciliation is a process based on two parties working together to heal a relationship.

Gospel-shaped grandparenting means that you forgive your family member as the Lord has forgiven you (Colossians 3:13). How does God forgive us? God forgives us unconditionally, completely, and sacrificially. The same grace that has been extended to you is to be extended *by* you. We like it when grace is given to us, but it is a lot harder when grace needs to be given by us. If you struggle with unforgiveness, meditate on God's grace and mercy from passages such as Psalm 51. When we understand how much we have been forgiven by God, we are better able to forgive others.

As a pastor, I'm involved in a lot of counseling situations, and an unwillingness to forgive is common. For example, I recently was officiating a wedding and saw firsthand the outcome of unwillingness to forgive. I was explaining to the groom how he would seat his grandparents and then his parents during the processional, and he stopped me. The groom said, "My grandparents and parents no longer talk to each other. Can I seat my grandparents somewhere else?" This is a Christ-loving, Bible-believing family, and they have their relational practices all wrong.

In another example, Jim's family attended the church where I was a pastor. His children were in my ministry, but I had never met him. One day he walked in and asked to meet with me. For sixty minutes, through many tears, he walked through a decade of bitter conflict with his former wife and his desire to have an intimate relationship with his children. He was desperate and asked what he should do. I bet you can guess what I told him: "Admit your mistakes and ask your ex-wife to forgive you." His response:

"Not until she does it first." Today he is a mad and a miserable man who has no relationship with his family.

I don't want you to experience what either of these families experienced. There is a direct correlation between the state of the relationship with your family and your willingness to forgive and ask for forgiveness. Forgiveness is the first step to restoring a relationship; it's an act that can change your family.

Imitate me

Young people are hard-wired to learn by example. Grandchildren watch our lives and absorb our passions and priorities. I love fishing, camping, bonfires, and the outdoors because my father and grandfather loved these hobbies. My grandparents modeled faithfulness in marriage, a deep faith in God, and the priority of local church involvement. These same passions and priorities were passed on to my father, who passed them on to me. These topics were talked about regularly in our family, but what cemented their place in my heart was the combination of teaching and example.

The Bible warns that the sin of a father often becomes the sin of a family for multiple generations (2 Kings 17:41). Grandparents who live in rebellion to God and do not walk in His ways may influence future generations to follow a similar path (Psalm 103:17; Exodus 34:6–7). The multigenerational examples from Scripture are sobering, but are meant to motivate us to a life of holiness.

Grandparents, as with every member of the family, are called to hate what is evil and cling to what is good (Romans 12:9), live in obedience to Christ, and flee from all impurity. Scripture sounds a loud warning to grandparents when it states, "Their fathers forgot my name" and "have not obeyed my words" (Jeremiah 23:27; 25:8). Romans 6:12 is an important priority for all grandparents: "Let not sin therefore reign in your mortal body." These passages remind us that God never allows us to sin successfully. Sin has consequences for ourselves and future generations.

Grandparents are called to model godliness before children and grandchildren. Grandparents can model how to live for Christ, make wise decisions, respond to suffering, and number our days (Psalm 90:12).

Grandparents who are serious about passing on faith to grandchildren must live in obedience to God and encourage future generations to do the same while warning them of the consequences of sin.

You should live a life that is worthy of imitation. Do your grandchildren see that you genuinely want to please the Lord? Do they see that when you fall short of God's standard there is a broken and contrite heart? The combination of Christlike character and heartfelt confession will impact your family.

If you cannot, with full integrity, say to your family right now, "Imitate me as I imitate Christ," then I encourage you to bring your sin before God. Sin withers only when the Gospel is brought to bear on it. Thomas Chalmers states,

> There is not one personal transformation in which the heart is left without an object of ultimate beauty and joy. The heart's desire for one particular object can be conquered, but its desire to have some object is unconquerable. The only way to dispossess the old heart of an object of affection is by the expulsive power of a new one.[1]

Sin can only be conquered when Jesus is savored as more beautiful and satisfying than the sin. The Gospel motivates us to say no to sin rather than feel that "I can sin because I will be forgiven later." We hate sin because God died for it.

Christianity has to be so real in your life that it changes the way you live. Let me give you an example from my life. My father used to take my brothers and me to northern Minnesota to fish for a week every summer. For eight hours a day for an entire week we would throw eight-inch lures through the water to try to catch a muskie. It takes 10,000 casts to catch one, they say. I've only caught a couple in my entire life.

On this particular day, we had fished for four straight hours. My arms were tired. I was hungry and I was giving my dad some teenager attitude. I remember my dad telling me to cast over by a submerged rock. In anger, I cast backward over my shoulder without looking and started to reel in. Then *bam!* I had hooked what turned out to be the biggest fish of my life up to that point—a 38½-inch muskie. We got the fish in the boat and were giving high fives and celebrating. Then came the inevitable question, "Can I keep it?"

Muskie at the time had to be a minimum of 40 inches to keep them. An inch and a half longer than my fish. I tried all my persuasive skills: "Come on, Dad, it's only an inch. We've been fishing for this fish for *years*. Who knows if we will ever catch another one?"

If this were you, what would you say to your child or grandchild? I can tell you what my dad said: "No. I'm sorry, Josh, we have to let it go." My dad gave me an incredible gift that day. I don't have a fish on the wall, but I have a love for honesty, in part because it was modeled for me. And two days later, God blessed my dad's integrity and he caught a 45-inch muskie that now hangs on his wall. Every time I see that fish it is a reminder, "Imitate me as I imitate Christ."

Paul says, "Conduct yourselves in a manner worthy of the gospel of Christ" (Philippians 1:27 NIV). Are you walking in a manner worthy of the Gospel? An authentic life, lived in passionate pursuit of Jesus Christ, is a powerful example for your family.

For the Sake of the Gospel

The fourth statement that can transform your family is, "I have become all things to all people, that by all means I might save some. I do it all for the sake of the gospel" (1 Corinthians 9:22–23). Or said another way, I grandparent for the sake of the Gospel.

The older we get, the greater the tendency to be stubborn and stuck in our ways. We think people should accommodate us, especially in the age of entitlement. After all, we earned it from a lifetime of sacrifice and work. Right? However, the Gospel turns that kind of thinking on its head.

- For the sake of the Gospel, become all things to all family members.
- For the sake of the Gospel, learn new technology.
- For the sake of the Gospel, flex on changes to family tradition.
- For the sake of the Gospel, be inclusive not exclusive.
- For the sake of the Gospel, what kind of accommodation needs to happen on behalf of your family?

You should be accommodating on matters of preference. Paul was willing to give up his preferences to win others to Christ, and I encourage grandparents to do the same with our families.

Finish this sentence as it relates to your children and grandchildren: "For the sake of the Gospel, I will _____."

In Jesus' Name, Amen

A Gospel-shaped grandparent is a praying grandparent because we recognize that we are powerless to change a heart and are completely dependent upon God. I am reminded of Paul's words in 1 Thessalonians 1:2, "We give thanks to God always for all of you, constantly mentioning you in our prayers."

The most powerful words you can ever say on behalf of your family are, "In Jesus' name, Amen." There are plenty of excuses not to pray, such as busyness, short attention span, or lack of desire. If you are not praying daily for your children, grandchildren, and future generations, then may these voices from the past encourage you to make prayer a priority.

- "God does nothing but by prayer, and everything with it." John Wesley

- "No duty is more earnestly impressed upon us in Scripture than the duty of continual communion with Him." David McIntyre
- "Prayer does not fit us for the greater work; prayer is the greater work." Oswald Chambers
- "Prayer is the forerunner of mercy. Turn to sacred history, and you will find that scarcely ever did a great mercy come to this world unheralded by supplication." Charles Spurgeon
- "Next to the wonder of seeing my Savior will be, I think, the wonder that I made so little use of the power of prayer." D. L. Moody
- "The greatest tragedy in life is not unanswered prayer, but unoffered prayer." F. B. Meyer
- "The devil is aware that one hour of close fellowship, hearty converse with God in prayer, is able to pull down what he hath been contriving and building many a year." John Flavel
- "There is no way that Christians, in a private capacity, can do so much to promote the work of God and advance the kingdom of Christ as by prayer." Jonathan Edwards
- "As it is the business of tailors to make clothes, and the business of cobblers to mend shoes, so it is the business of Christians to pray!" Martin Luther
- "Search for a person who claims to have found Christ apart from someone else's prayer, and your search may go on forever." E. Bauman

Blessed is the grandchild who has a praying grandparent. What families need today are not new and novel methods, but people who are mighty in prayer. God is able to do immeasurably more than we imagine. Through prayer God can transform the hardest heart or restore the most challenging relationship.

I'll end with a question. What difference does the Gospel make to grandparenting? It makes all the difference. It's your map and your mirror. When you wonder what to do as a grandparent, look to the Gospel. I have provided you with five statements based on the Gospel that can transform your family. As God did for you through Christ, go and do likewise for your family.

Grand Chat

1. What are the biggest grandparenting challenges you have faced? What encouragement can you give to others about how you navigated these challenges?

2. Which child or grandchild needs to hear "I love you" or words of affirmation from you today? If comfortable, share with the group.

3. Are there any relational tensions or barriers with your children or grandchildren that the group can pray for today?

4. In what areas of life have you learned to be accommodating to the needs of your family? Complete this sentence: "For the sake of the Gospel I will _____."

5. Share prayer needs with the group and end in a time of prayer.

16

Grandparent Declaration

Now that we have explored the cultural messages about grand-parenting, the biblical role of grandparents, and God's methods of discipleship in greater depth, the big question is this: Will you wholeheartedly embrace and faithfully steward the role God has given you as a grandparent? I don't want you to answer yes out of obligation or due to an emotional response. I want you to be honest with yourself, because making a promise to God and others is a big deal. Matthew 5:37 reminds us to "Let what you say be simply 'yes' or 'no.'"

With that said, I urge you to embrace God's role for grandparenting with the intention of keeping your promise.

Larry Fowler, founder of the Legacy Coalition and a good friend, wrote a grandparenting declaration that I encourage you to read carefully, and if God impresses it on your heart to do so, I encourage you to commit to it and sign your name at the bottom.[1]

I am a grandparent, and this is my declaration.

Yes, I am a grandparent,
But I am more than a grandparent,
I am a Christian grandparent.

I believe in the Bible and the God of the Bible.
I have received the grace of the Gospel of the Christ of the
Bible.
And I desire to be a lifelong devoted disciple.
I want my grandchildren to do the same!

Yes, I am a Christian grandparent. But I am more than that;
I am an intentional Christian grandparent, and this is my
declaration.

I love my grandkids, so
I will hold them when they're born,
Cuddle them when they're one,
Chase them when they're two,
Read to them when they're three,
Play with them when they're four,
And laugh at their jokes when they're five.

I'll support them,
Exhort them,
Cheer them,
Revere them,
I'll praise them, even
Help raise them—
I will be there for them!
But that's not enough.

As an intentional Christian grandparent,
I will do more!
I will pass on my faith.
But my vision is even beyond that:
I will perpetuate my faith.

Therefore, I will teach two generations.
But I will not only teach two generations,
I will think four generations.

I will ponder, "What kind of grandparent must I be
So my grandchild becomes one like me—
And then his carries on the legacy?"

Yes, I am an intentional Christian grandparent.
Culture says, "Retire and go play."
I say, "No thanks, I'll pray."
Culture says, "Pursue affluence."
I say, "I'll pursue influence."
Culture says, "You're old—you did your time."
I say, "Not so, I'm in my prime."
Culture says, "Those young generations—you can't relate."
I say, "Ain't true—my influence is great!"

I know my grandchildren need me.
But from me they need godly wisdom,
My Christlike example,
My faith stories,
My earnest prayers,
My uninterrupted time,
My unconditional love,
And my God-authorized blessing.

So what is intentional Christian grandparenting?
Let me spell it out for you . . .

I will   Guide grandchildren with grace.
I will   Respect parent roles.
I will   Abound in my affection.
I will   Nurture their nature.
I will   Deal with the dilemma of distance.
I will   Pray with passion and purpose.
I will   Adjust my attitude, in case I need to
            Restore relationships.
I will   Excel in my example.
I will   Number my days.
I will   Tell them my testimony.
I will   Intentionally influence.
I will   Never neglect the newest generation. Most importantly,
I will   Give them the gospel.

Because
I am an intentional Christian grandparent.

Name: _____

Date: _____

CONCLUSION

Final Thoughts

God designed grandparents to be disciple-makers who pass on a rich heritage of faith in Christ to future generations. Grandparents are partners with parents to raise the next generations to know, love, and serve God.

You have a decision to make. Will you be like Grandmother Lois and leave a lasting legacy of faith for future generations, or will you be like the rich man who said to himself, "You have plenty of grain laid up for many years. Take life easy; eat, drink, and be merry" (2 Timothy 1:5; Luke 12:19 NIV)? A Lois legacy or a life of ease, that is the choice before you.

We live at a time when many people have a low view of grand-parenting. Our culture has taken something that God designed to strengthen families and transmit faith and minimized it so that a Gospel-rich impact is neutralized. Our culture tells grandparents to live an independent life from family so as not to interfere or be a burden. The culture tells grandparents that they have worked hard and a season of self-indulgence is deserved. Culture tells grandparents to be a playmate and companion who spoils grandchildren. Grandparents must reject these messages.

God has given grandparents a ministry of first importance. It is critical that grandparents step into the biblical role God has given them. Your children and grandchildren need your godly influence in their lives. Families gain something of immeasurable value when you are active and engaged. Your Christlike example, biblical teaching, God-centered testimony, godly wisdom, and faithful prayers point grandchildren to Christ and make an eternal difference in their lives.

The Bible has much to say about the spiritual influence of grandparents. Passages such as Deuteronomy 4:9; 6:2–8; and Psalm 78:1–8 explain God's role for grandparents and biblical methods to pass on faith. Grandparents should adopt this attitude: "O God, from my youth you have taught me, and I still proclaim your wondrous deeds. So even to old age and gray hairs, O God, do not forsake me, until I proclaim your might to another generation, your power to all those to come" (Psalm 71:17–18).

Grandparenting matters, as I hope I have shown you in this book. Grandparents who are disciple-makers are difference-makers. I hope this book encourages you to be active and intentional in the lives of your family, to think multigenerationally, to live obediently, to pray fervently, to teach biblical truth confidently, to tell of the glory of God passionately, and to be a disciple-maker who passes on a rich heritage of faith to future generations.

I will end this book with "A Blessing for Grandparents"[1] in the hope that you will be a blessing to your family, church, and community.

A Blessing for Grandparents

Like Abraham, may you know God intimately
and be His friend;
Like Jeremiah, may you be gripped with a clear
sense of God's calling on your life;
May He empower you as He did Joshua and
Deborah;
May He guide you and provide for you as He did
for Ruth;
May He, in His providence, strategically use you
as He did Daniel and Esther for His great
glory;
Like Ezekiel, when your mission is completed,
may your family know that one of God's
spokespersons has been among them.
Like the disciples, may you make disciples of all
nations beginning with your children and your
children's children.
And like grandmother Lois, may you pass on a
heritage of faith to future generations.
May the Lord bless you and keep you and make
His face to shine upon you for Jesus' sake.

What Is the Responsibility of a Grandchild to a Grandparent?

Grandchildren, like grandparents, have a God-ordained role in the family. God provides clear instructions and has expectations for all members of the family. The primary role of a grandchild is to honor grandparents, which includes the responsibility to respect and care for you. I have provided a few talking points for family discussion.

Honor: "Honor your father and your mother" (Exodus 20:12).

- Honor is the central responsibility for grandchildren to grandparents, which has many applications.
- The word *honor* means to reverence, hold in awe, and value at a high price.
- Proverbs 23:22 provides an example of honor being put into action: "Listen to your father who gave you life, and do not despise your mother when she is old."
- Honor is demonstrated by positive action on behalf of the old—meeting their needs, listening to their advice,

recognizing their worth, and doing so in all sorts of ways large and small (1 Timothy 5:1; Leviticus 19:32; Proverbs 23:22).

- All grandparents are to be esteemed by grandchildren, but special honor is to be given to those who live godly lives.
- The Bible illustrates a number of ways in which grandparents can be honored: devotion (Ruth 1:16); financial support, especially for widows (Acts 6:1–4; 1 Timothy 5:3–8); providing a caring fellowship (Acts 2:42–26); and listening to the advice and wisdom of elders (1 Timothy 5:17–18). In Matthew 15:1–6, Jesus interprets the commandment "Honor your father and your mother" as referring to financial support.

Respect: "You shall stand up before the gray head and honor the face of an old man, and you shall fear your God: I am the Lord" (Leviticus 19:32).

- Standing is a sign of respect. It means to give weight to prominent people.
- The Bible values old age and gray hair, and speaks of these accomplishments as a blessing that deserves respect.
- We must not be infatuated with youth. We need more gray heads among us to learn from their wisdom and experience. New is not improved, and old is not obsolete.
- This passage encourages children and grandchildren to grant full significance to older generations because God granted long life as a blessing, often to those who were righteous and pleasing to Him as well as for what they have accomplished as the instructors of younger generations.

Care: "If anyone does not provide for his relatives, and especially for members of his household, he has denied the faith and is worse than an unbeliever" (1 Timothy 5:8).

- Children and grandchildren are to care for the needs of aging parents and grandparents. Family members are to look after the whole of aging members' lives, which includes food, clothing, and lodging as well as other needs.

- During the first half of a person's life, the parents give everything they have to supply the needs of their children. When they get to the point in life when they are no longer able to meet their own needs, it becomes the responsibility of their children and grandchildren to take care of them. This is one of God's ways of making families stick together. Parents raise children, and when the children are grown, they take care of their parents.

- Children and grandchildren are God's retirement plan, as they are to care for aging parents.

A word of caution if your family does not live as the Bible describes: It is never wise to demand action or demean behavior. Graciously share your feelings and point your family to the Bible. Talk about future scenarios with your family and come up with a shared plan that all members feel good about.

Finishing Well

A Sermon for Every Grandparent

God gave us passages like 2 Timothy 4:6–8 because we are prone to lose focus and chase after things that have no eternal value. Passages like these are soul-jarring, Jesus-exalting, and priority-clarifying. We all need to be reminded from time to time what really matters and how we are to use our days.

The Bible tells us that life is like a blade of grass and a vapor. It is short. It won't be long before our final day is here. I want to be prepared for the day I meet the Lord, and I want you to be prepared as well. I encourage you to consider the end of your days. For some, it will cause a change of direction, for we would not long pursue our present course if we are forced to gaze into the future.

2 Timothy 4:6–8

Second Timothy is the last book Paul wrote. He is an old man in prison—probably a hole in the ground or a cave—and he is awaiting his execution. Most commentators believe 2 Timothy was written only weeks or months before Paul's beheading by emperor Nero. Paul may have been lonely, as everyone but Luke has deserted him.

Second Timothy contains Paul's last recorded words. There is no pity party going on. I hear hope and joy in Paul's words. No resignation to call it quits; still a ton of fight left in the man. But the reality is, Paul knows his time is short and wants to finish strong. Paul offers a great example of how to face death and how to orient one's life to finish well.

What helped Paul finish his life well?

Five things helped Paul finish his life well:

1. Paul viewed his life as a sacrifice unto God (2 Timothy 4:6). Paul referred to himself as a "drink offering." What is a drink offering?[1]

Let's read Numbers 28:4, 7–8 as a reference point: "The one lamb you shall offer in the morning, and the other lamb you shall offer at twilight. . . . Its drink offering shall be a quarter of a hin for each lamb [1 to 2 quarts]. In the Holy Place you shall pour out a drink offering of strong drink to the Lord . . . with a pleasing aroma to the Lord."

Paul is making a reference to sacrifice and saying he is like the drink offering we just read about. Paul is saying that he lived his life as a sacrificial offering to Jesus. Or in other words, Paul lived a life of selfless service to God. Just as the drink offering was poured out on the altar, so Paul has been poured out for God. That is a powerful image, isn't it? And we are told this is a pleasing aroma to God.

A drink offering in the Old Testament comes alongside the main sacrifice. The main offering was a lamb, bull, or dove. Blood was shed and was accompanied by a drink offering. Can you see the point Paul is making? Paul was pointing out that Jesus is the main sacrifice—He is the lamb who shed His blood for the sins of people. Jesus spoke to this directly in Luke 22:20, emphasis added:

He picked up a cup of wine and said, "This cup that is *poured out* for you is the new covenant in my blood." The phrase "poured out" was not by chance or mistake. Jesus' sacrifice fulfilled the need of a drink offering, His blood literally pouring out when the soldier pierced His side with a spear (John 19:34).

Let's tie this back to finishing well. Paul knew his place. He was a drink offering, not *the* offering. His role was to point to Christ. If a person has an inflated notion of their own importance, they will not finish well. Paul was not living for significance, but for sacrifice.

Paul could go to his grave satisfied because the purpose of his life was not self-focused or his own satisfaction, but sacrificial service to God. If you want to finish your life well, the first step is to identify what you are living for. The Bible contains numerous examples of individuals who sought their own satisfaction yet all they found was emptiness and regret.

One example is Proverbs 5:11: "At the end of your life you groan, when your flesh and body are consumed." Here a father is warning his son of the consequences of sexual sin and says that if you do not obey God you will regret it your whole life. You will groan, "Ohh . . . why did I do that?" We don't want to come to the end of our life groaning, looking back with regret at a lifetime of choices made to satisfy self.

The world's big lie is that we will be happy if we live for ourselves and do what we want to do. If we've bought into this lie, we will wake up tomorrow morning with the driving motivation to make ourselves happy. This may lead a child to disobey his parents because he thinks this will bring satisfaction. It may lead a husband to pursue a romantic relationship with a woman who is not his wife because he is seeking satisfaction. It may lead an elderly person to retire and make leisure the focus of his life because he thinks this will bring satisfaction.

Proverbs 5:11 will be the outcome for each of these people. They will groan with regret. The happiness they seek will elude them. What we see in Paul is that to finish well requires the glad assumption of sacrificial service to Jesus Christ. Do you believe that? Our greatest happiness is found in Christ himself.

There is not a day of your life that Christ does not claim as "mine!" God expects every day to be lived as a drink offering unto Him. What this boils down to is, who are you living for? Who do you get out of bed for each morning?

2. Paul had a correct view of death (2 Timothy 4:6). Paul says the "time of my departure has come."

The Greek word for *departure* is a fun word; it means that the anchor is up and the ship is away. It means that death doesn't end Paul's journey. His real adventure is just beginning. His ship is setting sail! It carries with it the idea that death is never a cessation, but a beginning.

Think about this for a moment. Here is the picture this paints: Life on this earth is like a ship at port where all the preparations are made for the real journey to come. I'm struck that so many of us go about our days consumed by what is temporal rather than what is eternal. As it does for Paul, at some point the time of our departure will come.

When I look at Paul, I see him facing death with confidence. Why? How? We can face death with confidence because

1. Our body is a tent. Tents are only for temporary living and are not comfortable long-term. The Bible says we groan for a new, perfect body. Doesn't that excite you—to get a new body that has no problems? We have that to look forward to.

2. We know what happens at death. Fear always surrounds not knowing or controlling the future. The Bible has told us what happens when we die. Four things:

   a. Our spirit leaves our body. When Jesus brought the daughter of Jairus back to life, we read in Luke 8:54-55 NIV, "He took her by the hand and said, 'My child, get up!' Her spirit returned, and at once she stood up." This means that a dead body is simply an empty shell; the spirit of a person has departed.

b. Immediately we are present with God. Paul says in 2 Corinthians 5:8 that he "would rather be away from the body and at home with the Lord."

c. We will receive our new body at the return of Christ. Paul said, "We will not be found naked"—without a body. (2 Corinthians 5:3; 1 Corinthians 15:50–57; 1 Thessalonians 4:16–18).

d. We appear before the judgment seat of Christ so that we may receive what is due for things done in the body whether good or bad (2 Corinthians 5:10). This does not concern salvation, but is regarding rewards for the stewardship of our life. People who do not believe in Jesus appear before the Great White Throne of judgment (Revelation 20:11–15).

3. **Eternal life with God awaits us.** I am reminded that Jesus himself was in anguish over His coming death, and sweat drops of blood as he approached that hour (Luke 22:39–46). I am not a masochist, so the act of dying is not something I'm particularly excited about. However, we do not have to fear death itself. Why?

Because salvation in Christ eliminates that fear and carries with it the promise of new life. In Jesus, death is the beginning of something wonderful, not the end of all that was good. This is why the apostle Paul can confidently say, "Death has been swallowed up in victory" (1 Corinthians 15:54 NIV). Jesus conquered death. It does not have the final word, as there is hope and triumph through Christ!

Departure has a second meaning. It is a Greek word that refers to the unyoking of an ox from a plow. Think with me for a moment about what an ox is used for: hard work—planting and harvesting.

Here is the picture we are given; Paul had been doing hard work but now is done. Death released him from that. Death is both the beginning of new life and the end of hard work.

A common problem is that many Christians have bought in to cultural norms about how they should spend the final years of their life—as a season to rest, play, and indulge themselves.

The later years of life are not meant to be a season of stagnation for the Lord. This is not the pattern I see in Scripture. God does not give senior discounts, nor does He have retirement homes. In fact, the Bible teaches that aging often increases one's potential contribution to God and others. In Psalm 92:12–15, the picture of a palm tree is used to make this point: "The righteous will flourish like a palm tree and grow like a cedar in Lebanon. They are planted in the house of the Lord; they flourish in the courts of our God. They still bear fruit in old age; they are ever full of sap and green, to declare that the Lord is upright; he is my rock, and there is no unrighteousness in him." Our later years are to be like those of a date palm tree, which bears hundreds of pounds of fruit well past 150 years of age. God expects our later years to be productive years for His sake. Age does not impair the fruit-bearing capabilities. It enhances it.

This is what I see with Paul. He bore fruit until the day of his death. In fact, this is the pattern of elderly people in the Bible. The Bible has nothing good to say about idleness (Proverbs 6:6–11) or about the idle people who expect others to provide for them (2 Thessalonians 3:6–15). At no point should idleness be a sought-for attribute of life, especially in one's later years. God used many individuals in the later third of their lives for His kingdom purposes. Moses, Caleb, and Anna are a few noteworthy examples. The biblical expectation is that older women will invest in younger women, and older men in younger men (Titus 2). The biblical pattern is for grandparents to teach their grandchildren to fear the Lord and walk in His ways (Deuteronomy 6:1–2). Old age brings some transitions, but decreasing responsibility is not one of them.

Rather than retire, a generation of elderly Christians needs to re-fire and use their last years for the glory of Jesus. John Piper's advice is excellent:

> Live now to make much of Christ. Measure everything by this: Will it help more people admire Jesus more intensely and treasure Jesus more deeply? . . . So, all you Boomers just breaking into Medicare, gird up your loins, pick up your cane, head for the gym, and get fit for the last lap. Fix your eyes on the Face at the finish line. There will be plenty of time for R and R in the Resurrection. For now, there is happy work to be done.[2]

What kind of life lived would cause Jesus to say to an elderly person, "Well done, good and faithful servant"? If the time of your departure has not come, then there is happy work to be done for the Lord.

4. Paul looked forward to standing before God, the righteous judge (2 Timothy 4:8). Nero had unjustly judged Paul, but Nero does not have the last word. Paul knew he would not be unjustly judged by Christ. Instead, the righteous Judge would vindicate him. Paul knew he could look forward to a reward—the crown of righteousness.

Verse 8 says that Jesus himself will give the crown of righteousness. What a great image. Let that sink in. God rewards those in Christ with His righteousness—that's what a crown of righteousness means. The crown we receive is Christ's righteousness, and it is the reward of eternal life with Christ. We are rewarded when we get to heaven, and this passage clarifies what that reward is. Paul could finish his life well because he knew what awaited him.

Two words that catch my attention in verse 8 are "that day." Are you living this day for that day? The day you stand before Jesus. How does the idea of standing before Jesus land on you? Does it produce anxiety or joy?

5. Paul finished well because he reproduced himself in others (2 Timothy 4:1–5). Dying is easier when one's life has not been wasted. Paul could face the twilight of life knowing that although he would die, his influence would continue to live on in the lives of those he impacted.

Look at verses 1–5. Here is a summary of the things Paul has been teaching Timothy. Paul could go to his grave because he had reproduced himself in Timothy, Titus, and many others. Paul's impact lived on even after his death because he invested in people.

Who have you reproduced yourself in? Who are you reproducing yourself in right now? Who are you discipling and helping to become more like Christ? If you were to die, who would show up at your funeral and say, "He or she made a difference in my life." Or maybe, "I love Jesus and walked with Jesus because of him." Or how about, "I'm a better husband or wife, mother or father, because of her."

Thinking about our end clarifies how to live our now. I think about death often—not because I want to die, but because there are few subjects like death that have the power to strip away the vanities of life and bring into focus what is to be our priority for living.

Every one of us faces a danger of wasting our days.

- Who are you living for—is your life an offering to God or a monument to yourself?
- Are you working for the Lord, or have you prematurely unhitched yourself from the ox?
- Does the idea of standing before the Lord produce anxiety or joy?
- Who are you reproducing yourself in right now?

Maybe one of those questions triggered something you realize you need to give some attention to.

Let us guard against the tendency to finish life poorly. The Bible is littered with individuals who did not finish well and whose love for Christ grew cold (Matthew 24:12). This fact should serve as a warning to us. It should be the desire of every one of us to say on his or her day of death, "I have fought the good fight, I have finished the race, I have kept the faith" (2 Timothy 4:7).

Appendix C:

Grandparenting Video Study Questions

Strengthening Your Family and Passing on Your Faith

GENERAL EDITOR JOSH MULVIHILL

_____ **Introduction** _____

Grandparenting is a one-of-a-kind video resource featuring eight family ministry experts and over six hours of video. This ten-session series is packed with powerful messages, sound biblical principles, and practical ideas to help Sunday school classes, small groups, churches, and grandparents intentionally influence grandchildren for Christ. Discussion questions are available in this appendix as well as online at gospelshapedfamily.com and legacycoalition.com.

The Legacy Coalition is an organization committed to equipping grandparents to reach and disciple grandchildren and helping churches to minister effectively to the millions of Christian grandparents who need encouragement, training, and resources. For more information, visit our website at legacycoalition.com.

Josh Mulvihill
Director of Resources | The Legacy Coalition

Why Establish a Grandparent Ministry?

Larry Fowler

Summary:

Christian grandparents have a tremendous potential to influence the hearts of their grandchildren, a potential second only to that of parents. Sadly, grandparents are overlooked, ignored, and mislabeled as being "old." The Church has not recognized what Scripture says about the role of grandparents or provided resources to equip them. Seven books, two video series, and one organization exist to support thirty-million Christian grandparents presently living in the United States. The Legacy Coalition is a movement committed to equipping and empowering grandparents and church leaders through networking, resourcing, and conferencing. You can join this movement by championing ministries for grandparents in your church.

Key Points:

- Grandparents are mandated by Scripture to pass on a spiritual legacy to future generations.
- Grandparents have the tremendous potential to minister to their grandchildren, second only to the parents.
- Grandparents are often overlooked, ignored, and mislabeled by their churches.
- Resources for Christian grandparents are extremely limited.
- The Legacy Coalition is committed to equipping and empowering grandparents and church leaders.

Key Passages:

Deuteronomy 4:9
Psalm 78

Discussion Questions:

1. What role did your grandparents have in your life?
2. How did you learn to be a grandparent?
3. Why do you think the church fails to recognize the importance of grandparents?
4. List the four reasons Larry Fowler mentioned for starting a grandparenting ministry at your church.
5. List specific steps you can take to establish a ministry for grandparents at your church.

What is the Biblical Role of a Grandparent?

Josh Mulvihill

Summary:

Every member of the family is given a God-ordained role that is not interchangeable with other family members. God gives husbands the role of sacrificial service as the head; wives are to willingly follow their husbands' leadership as a helpmate; children are told to honor authority; and grandparents are to leave a spiritual heritage to future generations. Unfortunately, American culture is ambiguous about the role of grandparents. The new social contract, described by Arthur Kornhaber, demands autonomy between the generations, leaves grandparents feeling disconnected, and encourages grandparents not to meddle in the lives of their adult children and grandchildren. The Bible instructs grandparents to leave a rich, godly heritage of faith to the fourth generation. God expects grandparents to tell their grandchildren about the work of the Lord and teach them His commands, so they will set their hope in Him and not stray from His path.

Key Points:

- Every member of the family is given a God-ordained role that is not interchangeable with other family members.
- The role of grandparents is ambiguous in American culture.
- The new social contract, described by Arthur Kornhaber, demands autonomy between the generations.
- According to Dr. Elmer Towns, the most important thing grandparents can leave their grandchildren is a godly heritage.
- Scripture instructs grandparents to tell their grandchildren about the works of God and to teach them His commands.

Key Passages:

Ephesians 5:25–31

Genesis 2:18

Exodus 20:12

Psalm 78:1–8

Discussion Questions:

1. Evaluate your understanding of the role of grandparents. Do your actions reflect a biblical or cultural view? What changes do you need to make?

2. What are your goals for your grandchildren? How do these align with the goals of salvation and sanctification from Psalm 78?

3. What "gems of faith" can you share with your grandchildren? (For example, how has God answered prayer and provided for you?)

4. Discuss practical ways to tell your grandchildren about the work of the Lord and teach His commands.

How to Pass Faith to Future Generations

Cavin Harper

Summary:

A moral chasm threatens the hearts and minds of children. Therefore, it is imperative that grandparents tell grandchildren the whole truth about Jesus. Grandparents should teach grandchildren who Jesus is according to Scripture: a baby born in Bethlehem, a compassionate and loving friend, a suffering servant, the Lion of Judah, a righteous Judge, a jealous God, and an all-consuming fire. Grandparents make a difference when they incorporate at-home moments, on-the-go opportunities, wake-up rituals, and bedtime blessings to pass a spiritual legacy to their grandchildren. Grandparents make a difference when they embrace God's mandate to disciple their grandchildren—intentionally speaking blessings into their lives, engaging them in the stories of God's marvelous works, and telling them the whole truth about Christ.

Key Points:

- Grandparents are mandated by Scripture to tell their grandchildren the whole truth about Jesus.
- Grandparents influence their grandchildren by speaking blessings into their lives and telling them the stories of God's marvelous works.
- Deuteronomy 6:4–9 provides grandparents a template for passing a spiritual legacy to future generations.
- Grandparents need to embrace a multigenerational view of family.

Key Passages:

Psalm 78:1–8

Judges 2:10–12

Deuteronomy 4:9

Deuteronomy 6:4–9

Discussion Questions:

1. Discuss the difference between a "teddy bear" image of Christ and the true image of Christ.

2. Read Judges 2:10–12. Why did Joshua's grandchildren wander far from God? How could this tragedy have been prevented?

3. Describe the ways you have attempted to "show-and-tell" the person of Jesus.

4. Discuss ways to incorporate at-home moments, on-the-go opportunities, wake-up rituals, and bedtime blessings for intentionally passing a spiritual legacy to your grandchildren.

5. How can you encourage your pastor and church to embrace a multigenerational view of family?

Loving Grandkids in Scary Times

Valerie Bell

Summary:

With words like *Columbine* and *Sandy Hook* generating terror, it's no wonder safety is the number-one issue for parents and grandparents. However, grandparents should want more for their grandchildren than physical safety. Grandparents optimize their days by growing in their own faith and trusting their grandchildren to God, as well as making sure their grandchildren are equipped with spiritual tools and knowing how to use them. Most important, grandparents should make sure their grandchildren understand that God will never leave them nor forsake them.

Key Points:

- Grandparents are uniquely positioned to point their grandchildren to Christ.
- Grandparents must provide their grandchildren with spiritual tools and model how to use them.
- Grandparents must teach their grandchildren that God redeems their messes and will never leave them nor forsake them.
- Grandchildren may be more receptive to the supernatural possibilities of God than most adults.
- God always writes the last chapter.

Key Passages:

1 Samuel 3

Psalm 23

Matthew 6:9–13

Discussion Questions:

1. What things scare you the most about the times in which we live?
2. What tools are you using to strengthen your own faith in Christ?
3. What spiritual tools are you offering your grandchildren? How are you teaching them to use them?
4. Practice saying the knuckle prayer so you are prepared to teach it to your grandchildren.
5. Have you witnessed God creating beauty from your messes, your children's messes, or your grandchildren's messes? If so, cite specific examples.

——— Never Too Late: Encouraging Faith in Your Adult Children ———

Rob Rienow

Summary:

Statistics reveal that a high number of young adults are disconnected from their faith, church, and family. Two-thirds of Christian parents who have empty nests experience guilt from having at least one prodigal child. There is encouraging news, however. Parents are still in the position to influence the faith of their adult children by following four parenting principles found in Scripture: (1) offer their heart to God, (2) turn their heart toward their children, (3) draw their children's heart toward them, and (4) point their children's heart to Christ. Parents begin by confessing and repenting of their parenting mistakes. They ask God to turn their heart toward their adult children in a spirit of compassion as well as draw their children's heart toward them with warmth, honesty, and trust. Last, they ask God to give them the ability to share the Gospel message unashamedly.

Key Points:

- Parents' ultimate goal for their children is that they love God with their heart, trust Christ with their present and future, and arrive safely home.

- Parents are the shortest distance between the hearts of their adult children and Christ.

- Two-thirds of Christian parents experience guilt from having at least one child who has strayed from the faith.

- Parents must repent of their parenting mistakes and focus their prayers on the condition of their children's hearts.

- A powerful way for parents to build heart connections with their adult children is to ask forgiveness for their failures and to communicate fears about sharing their faith.

Key Passages:

Ezekiel 18

Malachi 4:6

Matthew 9:36

Proverbs 23:26

Romans 1:16

Isaiah 60:1–4

Discussion Questions:

1. How did your relationship with your children change when they became adults?
2. Do your actions reflect the belief that you are totally, partially, or not at all responsible for your children's choices?
3. How are your children connected to or disconnected from their faith, church, and family?
4. What spiritual battles are your children facing?
5. List the four parenting principles mentioned by Rob Rienow. How can you use these principles to encourage your prodigal child to accept Christ as Lord and Savior?

Grandparenting Through a Child's Divorce

Linda Ranson Jacobs

Summary:

Parents have to face the reality of their child's divorce. They begin by giving themselves permission to grieve the death of a marriage, broken dreams, and loss of relationships. They need to be aware that their grandchildren may suffer torn loyalties. Their grandchildren will manifest the impact of the suffering differently, depending on their ages. God has placed grandparents in the family for "such a time as this" (Esther 4:14), to provide a safe, empathetic environment, rich in rituals and traditions, where grandchildren are free to express their pain. Grandparents help grandchildren survive divorce, so the pattern of divorce is not repeated through the generations.

Key Points:

- Grandparents grieve the death of a marriage and the loss of relationships when their adult child divorces.
- Grandparents are in the position to offer their grandchildren a safe environment, removed from the divorce battle zone.
- Divorce may cause grandchildren to suffer torn loyalties between their parents.
- Rituals are the emotional glue that holds the relationship with grandchildren together.
- Divorce is cyclical.

Key Passages:

Malachi 2:16

Psalm 23

Esther 4:14

Discussion Questions:

1. What impact has divorce had on your life or the lives of your family members?
2. Discuss the ways divorce impacts children of different ages.
3. List the do's and don'ts of helping your grandchildren during divorce.
4. In what ways are you the "safe-keeper" for your grandchildren?
5. Discuss the importance of rituals and traditions in your family. Give specific examples.
6. In what ways can you minister to the divorced families in your congregation?

—————————— **The Art of Single Grandparenting** ——————————

Cathy Jacobs

Summary:

Single grandparents have the difficult challenge of being alone. They simultaneously juggle multiple tasks such as baby-sitting, cooking, and entertaining, without the help of a grandparent companion. Grandmothers whose husbands have abdicated their role as grandfathers face a similar challenge. Widowed grandparents face the unique struggle of unexpected grief, which accompanies life's milestones such as the birth of a grandchild. Scripture reminds us that regardless of our circumstances, Christ came to bind the brokenhearted and to set the captive free. The church can assist by investing in the lives of all grandparents, building a community that provides fellowship, support, and a sense of purpose.

Key Points:

- Three types of single grandparents exist: divorcees, widows/widowers, and women whose husbands are absentee grandfathers.
- Single grandparents have the difficult challenge of being alone.
- God graciously fills the lives of the widowed and divorced with grandchildren.
- Christ came to bind the brokenhearted and to set the captive free.
- God turns our messes into messages of redemption.

Key Passages:

2 Corinthians 1:3–4

Colossians 3:13

Isaiah 61:1–3

Revelation 21:4

Discussion Questions:

1. What struggles are unique to single grandparents? How can the church support or encourage single grandparents?

2. Would your grandchildren describe their grandfather as active or absent in their life? Explain.

3. Discuss ways your church can build community among grandparents.

4. Where are you in the journey between an encrusted acorn and a glorious oak tree?

5. How has God turned your mess into your message?

Passing on a Heritage of Faith with Enthusiasm and Joy

Lynda Freeman

Summary:

Grandparents must get their grandchildren's attention in order to pass on a faith legacy. The key to getting grandchildren's attention is discovering who they are and what makes them tick. Are they creative or logical? Do they like to tinker or read? Grandparents gain their grandchildren's attention, so they remember God's Word, understand it, live it, and experience changed lives. Grandchildren are more receptive to God's Word when grandparents invest in their lives and openly praise God for their identities as His handiwork. Opportunities for passing a legacy of faith to grandchildren include reading and discussing books, participating in service projects, creating prayer journals, carrying out science projects, and watching for God's blessings in their lives. If grandchildren don't develop their own walk with God, they will eventually forget Him.

Key Points:

- Grandparents need to gain their grandchildren's attention, so they remember God's Word, understand it, live it, and experience changed lives.
- Grandparents need to invest in their grandchildren's lives and let them know they are the handiwork of God.
- Grandparents can pass on a legacy of faith to their grandchildren by reading and discussing books, participating in service projects, creating prayer journals, and carrying out science projects.
- Grandchildren need to develop their own walk with God; otherwise, they will eventually forget Him.

Key Passages:

Psalm 78:1–8

Psalm 139:13–14

1 Thessalonians 5:16–18

Discussion Questions:

1. List three adjectives that describe your grandchildren.
2. List three activities that get your grandchildren's attention and capture their imagination.
3. Discuss service projects you and your grandchildren can participate in together.
4. How do you model prayer for your grandchildren?
5. What activities have you discovered that help your grandchildren connect with God?

How to Pray and Read the Bible with Your Grandchildren

Rob Rienow

Summary:

Family is God's primary vehicle for reaching the hearts of children and grandchildren for Christ. Reformation churches radically committed to global evangelism recognize that faith begins in the home. A shift from "home-centered, church-supported" to "church-centered, home-supported" evangelism and discipleship occurred in the twentieth century. Today, only 5 percent of churchgoing families have a regular time for daily prayer and Bible reading. The challenge is to start somewhere. The strongest family worship curriculum available is reading Scripture with a believing heart. The worship toolbox also contains activities, songs, discussions, prayer, and catechism. Satan will target the efforts of parents and grandparents, because the two most important relationships—the vertical relationship with God and the horizontal relationship with family—intersect with family worship.

Key Points:

- Family is God's primary vehicle for evangelizing and discipling children and grandchildren.
- Five percent (1 in 20) of churchgoing families have a regular time for daily family worship.
- Family worship is the intersection between right relationships with God and family.
- Family worship is a key target of the enemy.
- Family worship includes activity, singing, Bible reading, discussion, prayer, and catechism.
- The strongest curriculum available is reading the Bible with a believing heart.

Key Passages:

Deuteronomy 4:9

Deuteronomy 6:4–9

Judges 2:6–11

Psalm 78:1–8

Hebrews 4:12

Discussion Questions:

1. Discuss the effects of the twentieth-century shift from "home-centered, church-supported" to "church-centered, home-supported" evangelism and discipleship.

2. Who reached your heart for Christ? If comfortable, please share details.

3. What did family worship look like when you were a child? What did family worship look like when you raised your children? What does family worship look like for your grandchildren?

4. Discuss the ideas in the family worship toolbox that appeal to you. Discuss the ones that seem unappealing.

5. What steps can you take toward developing or improving the quality of family worship in your home?

6. Pray for the salvation and sanctification of your family.

Unleashing the Power of Spoken Blessing

Cavin Harper

Summary:

A grandparent's words have the potential to bless or curse. The spoken blessing serves as a conduit through which grandparents affirm their grandchildren's worth as children of God. While prayers are spoken to God on behalf of grandchildren, blessings are spoken to grandchildren on behalf of God. There are two types of blessings: a general (recurring) blessing, such as the Levitical or Aaronic blessing (Numbers 6:24–26), and a personal (specific) blessing that occurs during life's milestones. The Levitical blessing beautifully communicates God's protection, pleasure, and peace. Spoken blessing consists of three critical elements: communicating high value, picturing a special future, and declaring our active commitment. A blessing is accompanied by a form of meaningful touch, such as a hand placed on the shoulder. Speaking blessings into the lives of grandchildren is critical to their spiritual health and well-being.

Key Points:

- Words have the potential to bless or curse.
- God is the source of blessing, with parents and grandparents as His conduits.
- Prayers are addressed to God on behalf of others; blessings are addressed to others on behalf of God.
- The purpose of the blessing is to boost a child's self-worth (not self-esteem).
- Three elements of the spoken blessing are communicating high value, picturing a special future, and making an active commitment.
- Two types of blessings include general (recurring) blessings and personal (specific) blessings.
- A father's blessing is critical.

Key Passages:

Genesis 1:27–29

Deuteronomy 6:7

Numbers 6:22–26

Matthew 3:17; Mark 1:11; Luke 3:22

Discussion Questions:

1. Words from a grandparent have the potential to bless or curse. If possible, site personal examples for each.

2. Discuss the difference between self-worth and self-esteem.

3. Discuss the difference between prayers and blessings.

4. What part of the Levitical blessing spoke loudest to you?

5. Discuss specific opportunities you have to speak blessings into the lives of your children and grandchildren.

6. Write a spoken blessing for each of your grandchildren. Be sure to include the following elements: high value, special future, and active commitment.

NOTES

Introduction

1. I've researched and written extensively about this in my book *Biblical Grandparenting*.

Chapter 1: Influencing Grandchildren for Christ

1. To learn more about the research, see Dr. Josh Mulvihill, *Biblical Grandparenting: Exploring God's Design for Disciple-Making and Passing Faith to Future Generations* (Bloomington, MN: Bethany House Publishers, 2018), 173–184.

2. Barna Group, "Teen Role Models: Who They Are, Why They Matter," 2011, www.barna.org/barna-update/millennials/467-teen-role-models#.V6tVFjqdLzI.

Chapter 2: Recognizing Culture's Role for Grandparents

1. "Old Age Intestate," *Harper's Magazine* 162, May 1931, 717.

2. Billy Graham, *Nearing Home: Life, Faith, and Finishing Well* (Nashville, TN: Thomas Nelson, 2013), 42.

3. "The Retirement City: A New Way of Life for the Old," *Time* magazine, August 1962, accessed October 5, 2012, www.time.com/time/magazine/article/0,9171,896472,00.html.

4. Andrew D. Blechman, *Leisureville: Adventures in a World without Children* (New York: Grove, 2008), 32.

5. Carol Shammas, Marylynn Salmon, and Michel Dahlin, *Inheritance in America: From Colonial Times to the Present* (New Brunswick, NJ: Rutgers University Press, 1987), 160.

6. Blechman, *Leisureville*, 4–5.

7. Blechman, *Leisureville*, 12.

8. Blechman, *Leisureville*, 17.

9. Annette Witheridge, "Ten Women to Every Man, a Black Market in Viagra, and a 'Thriving Swingers Scene': Welcome to The Villages, Florida," *Daily Mail*, June 16, 2014, http://www.dailymail.co.uk/news/article-2657325 /Ten-women-man-black-market-Viagra-thriving-swingers-scene-Welcome -The-Villages-Florida-elderly-residents-Sex-Square-cocktail-honor-woman -68-arrested-public-sex-toyboy.html.

10. Stefanie Cohen, "Romance and STDs: Inside Florida's Wild Retirees Getaway," *New York Post*, January 25, 2009, http://nypost.com/2009/01/25 /retire-to-the-bedroom/.

11. Blechman, *Leisureville*, 5.

12. Arthur Kornhaber, *The Grandparent Solution: How Parents Can Build a Family Team for Practical, Emotional, and Financial Success* (San Francisco: Jossey-Boss, 2004), 33–34.

13. Gunhild O. Hagestad, "Continuity and Connectedness," in *Grandparenthood*, ed. V. Bengtson and J. Robertson (Beverly Hills, CA: Sage, 1985), 33.

14. Andrew J. Cherlin and Frank F. Furstenberg, *The New American Grandparent: A Place in the Family, a Life Apart* (Cambridge, MA: Harvard University Press, 1992), 74.

Chapter 3: Giving Season

1. "Peace Prayer of Saint Francis," https://www.loyolapress.com/our -catholic-faith/prayer/traditional-catholic-prayers/saints-prayers/peace -prayer-of-saint-francis.

2. Claire A. Etaugh and Judith S. Bridges, *Women's Lives: A Psychological Exploration*, 3rd ed (New York: Routledge, 2016), 196.

Chapter 6: What Is the Role of a Grandparent?

1. Rob Rienow, *Visionary Parenting* (Nashville: Randall House, 2009), 9.

2. Bill Hull, *The Complete Book of Discipleship: On Being and Making Followers of Christ* (Colorado Springs: Navpress, 2006), 114.

3. Hull, 25.

4. David Briggs, "The No. 1 Reason Teens Keep the Faith as Young Adults," *Huffington Post*, October 29, 2014, www.huffingtonpost.com/david -briggs/the-no-1-reason-teens-kee_b_6067838.html.

5. Paul and Diana Miller, *A Guide to Great Grandparenting* (Colorado Springs: The Christian Grandparent Network, 2017), 13.

6. Adapted from Bob Hostetler, "The Four Phases of Parenthood," Focus on the Family, http://www.focusonthefamily.com/parenting/parenting-roles /phases-of-parenthood.

7. Roy B. Zuck, *Precious in His Sight: Childhood & Children in the Bible* (Grand Rapids: Baker, 1996), 103.

8. James Faris, "Young People Also Need an Abundance of Counselors," April 12, 2017, http://gentlereformation.com/2017/04/12/young-people-also -need-an-abundance-of-counselors/.

9. James Faris, "Young People Also Need an Abundance of Counselors."

Chapter 7: God's Vision for Your Family from Psalm 78

1. Fanny J. Crosby, "Blessed Assurance," public domain.

Chapter 8: Three Deficiencies in Christian Families

1. Barna Group, "Parents Accept Responsibility for Their Child's Spiritual Development but Struggle with Effectiveness," May 5, 2003, www.barna.com /research/parents-accept-responsibility-for-their-childs-spiritual-develop ment-but-struggle-with-effectiveness/, accessed October 11, 2016.

2. Woodrow Kroll, "The New American and the New Bible Illiteracy," *Free Republic*, June 27, 2007, www.freerepublic.com/focus/f-religion/1857058 /posts.

3. Barna Group, "Barna Survey Examines Changes in Worldview Among Christians over the Past 13 Years," March 9, 2009, https://www.barna.com /research/barna-survey-examines-changes-in-worldview-among-christians -over-the-past-13-years/.

4. Larry Fowler, *The Question Nobody Asks About Our Children*, Awana Clubs International, 2014, http://k.b5z.net/i/u/6021236/f/the-question-nobody -asks-about-our-children.pdf, 11.

5. Jonathan Morrow, "Why Generation Z Is Less Christian than Ever— and Why That's Good News," *Fox News*, March 11, 2018, http://www.fox news.com/opinion/2018/03/11/why-generation-z-is-less-christian-than-ever -and-why-thats-good-news.html.

6. Jonathan Morrow, "Why Generation Z Is Less Christian than Ever."

Chapter 10: Discipleship Practices Every Grandparent Can Do (Part 1)

1. John Trent and Gary Smalley, *The Blessing: Giving the Gift of Uncon- ditional Love and Acceptance* (Nashville: Thomas Nelson, 2004), 30.

2. Trent and Smalley, 30.

3. Trent and Smalley, 30.

4. Trent and Smalley, 31.

5. Trent and Smalley, 34.

6. Sam Crabtree, *Practicing Affirmation: God-Centered Praise of Those Who Are Not God* (Wheaton: Crossway, 2011), 26.

7. Sylvia Gunter, *For the Family* (Birmingham: The Father's Business, 1994), 5.

8. Gunter, 5.

Chapter 11: Discipleship Practices Every Grandparent Can Do (Part 2)

1. Leigh Anderson, "How to Talk With Religious Conservatives About LBGT Rights," *Lifehacker*, July 13, 2017, https://lifehacker.com/how-to-talk-with-religious-conservatives-about-lgbt-rig-1796623461.

2. Anderson, "How to Talk With Religious Conservatives About LBGT Rights."

3. Adapted from Greg Gilbert, *What Is the Gospel?* (Wheaton, IL: Crossway, 2010).

Chapter 13: Developing Strong Relationships

1. Caryl Rivers and Rosalind C. Barnett, "Gray Divorce: Why Your Grandparents Are Finally Calling It Quits," *Los Angeles Times*, September 28, 2016, www.latimes.com/opinion/op-ed/la-oe-rivers-barnett-gray-divorce-20160928-snap-story.html.

2. Julie Zauzmer, "How Decades of Divorce Helped Erode Religion," *Washington Post*, September 27, 2016, www.washingtonpost.com/news/acts-of-faith/wp/2016/09/27/how-decades-of-divorce-helped-erode-religion/.

3. Linda Bloom and Charlie Bloom, "Overwhelmed Parents: A National Crisis," *Huffington Post*, May 25, 2013, www.huffingtonpost.com/linda-bloom-lcsw-and-charlie-bloom-msw/overwhelmed-parents-a-nat_b_330 8576.html.

4. Andy Crouch, *The Tech-Wise Family: Everyday Steps for Putting Technology in Its Proper Place* (Grand Rapids: Baker Books, 2017), 23.

5. Bloom and Bloom, "Overwhelmed Parents."

6. Susan Stiffelman, "Mom Overwhelmed by Endless To Do List," September 19, 2017, www.huffingtonpost.com/susan-stiffelman/mom-over whelmed-by-endles_b_12079728.html.

7. Rachel Martin, "Six Unspoken Truths for the Overwhelmed Mom," http://findingjoy.net/youre-overwhelmed-6-truths-motherhood-days/#.WY xwNnfMzeQ.

Chapter 14: Factors That Impact Relationships

1. Andrew J. Cherlin and Frank F. Furstenberg, *The New American Grandparent: A Place in the Family, a Life Apart* (Cambridge, MA: Harvard University Press, 1992), 16, 107.

2. Cherlin and Furstenberg, *The New American Grandparent*, 80.

Chapter 15: Gospel-Shaped Grandparenting

1. Thomas Chalmers, "The Expulsive Power of a New Affection," *Christianity Today*, March 2010, www.christianity.com/christian-life/spiritual-growth/the-expulsive-power-of-a-new-affection-11627257.html.

Chapter 16: Grandparent Declaration

1. Larry Fowler's grandparenting declaration is available online at https://legacycoalition.com/legacy-grandparenting-summit-the-grandparents-declaration/.

Conclusion: Final Thoughts

1. Adapted from a blessing by Dr. Paul Ferris, Bethel Seminary, St. Paul, MN, May 2008.

Appendix B: Finishing Well: A Sermon for Every Grandparent

1. Peter J. Leithart, "The Theology of the Drink Offering," *Biblical Horizons* 25, May 1991, www.biblicalhorizons.com/biblical-horizons/no-25-the-theology-of-the-drink-offering/.

2. John Piper, "What Happens When You Turn 65?" *Desiring God*, April 2011, www.desiringgod.org/articles/what-happens-when-you-turn-65.

Josh Mulvihill is the executive director of church and family ministry at Renewanation, where he equips parents and grandparents to disciple their family and consults with church leaders to help them design Bible-based, Christ-centered children's, youth, and family ministries. Josh has served as a pastor for nearly twenty years, is a founding member of the Legacy Coalition, and has a PhD from the Southern Baptist Theological Seminary. He is the author of *Biblical Grandparenting*, *Preparing Children for Marriage*, and *Rooted Kids Curriculum and Worship*. Josh and his wife, Jen, live in Victoria, Minnesota, and have five children. For family discipleship resources, visit GospelShapedFamily.com.

More Foundational Grandparenting Resources from Dr. Josh Mulvihill!

Ideal for pastors and church leaders, as well as for use in seminary classrooms, this insightful leadership book places grandparenting ministry on a firm scriptural foundation. This resource is perfect for helping you share how grandparents can invest spiritually in their grandkids and speak wisdom and godliness into their lives.

Biblical Grandparenting by Dr. Josh Mulvihill

With depth and relevance, this brief book for pastors offers practical guidance on how to begin a grandparenting ministry in your church. Discover tools and resources to help grandparents share their faith with and disciple a new generation.

Equipping Grandparents by Dr. Josh Mulvihill

Featuring eight family ministry experts and over six hours of video content, you will find all you need to invest spiritually in your grandkids in this DVD resource. Perfect for individual use, small groups, or Sunday school classes.

Grandparenting DVD

BETHANYHOUSE